KT-485-894

GIVE AND TAKE

Jack Gratus

BBC BOOKS

Published by BBC Books,
a division of BBC Enterprises Limited
Woodlands, 80 Wood Lane, London W12 0TT

First published 1990

ISBN 0 563 21534 8

Set in 10/11½ pt Times Roman by Goodfellow & Egan Ltd, Cambridge
Printed and bound in England by Clays Ltd, St Ives plc
Cover printed by Clays Ltd, St Ives plc

Contents

Introduction
Why this book?

'Oh, hell, not another meeting!'

'I've nothing but meetings all day! When am I going to do some work?'

To listen to the way some people talk, you could be forgiven for thinking that meetings have been devised as a punishment for dutiful and ambitious managers, and that nothing ever gets done at them. For some people the word itself conjures up memories of sitting for endless hours on uncomfortable chairs in small, smoky rooms, listening to bores droning on about totally irrelevant subjects to which no one pays attention.

The fact is, like them or not, meetings are an integral part of most people's working life. Surveys of organisations, large and small, show that approximately a quarter of a manager's time is spent at meetings. The number and length of meetings increase as you climb higher up the management scale until, at senior management level, you might be attending meetings almost four days out of five.

Meetings take place so often that we do not stop to work out how expensive they are. But, if you make a simple calculation of the average number of hours spent by, say, a middle manager in meetings per week, multiply this by his or her hourly average earnings and multiply that again by the number of middle managers in that company, you can quickly work out that the cost is in the thousands of pounds, if not hundreds of thousands. Unfortunately, many meetings are poorly chaired and those attending them do not know how to get the best out of them, so at least 50 per cent of the time is wasted. So the question that should be asked before and after every meeting is: was it worth it? If the answer is negative, that is one good reason for not holding a similar meeting again.

If the prospect of having to chair, or make a contribution to, a meeting daunts you then this book should be just right for you, because it is written specially for those whose jobs involve going to meetings, either as the Chair or as an ordinary member, but who feel that they are inhibited by lack of skill from making the most of them.

The shape of the book is owed to my career as a freelance journalist when I learnt that to give the story a focus, it was necessary to answer the five 'Ws', i.e. WHY, WHO, WHERE, WHEN and WHAT. I have done so by answering the following questions in Part One: Why have meetings? Who goes to meetings? Where and when do meetings take place? In Part Two the questions are: What happens at meetings? What happens when meetings go wrong? And what happens after the meetings are finished? Finally, under the heading, 'How did the meeting go?', there is a checklist for Chairs and members covering all the main aspects of running and attending meetings.

The single unifying theme of the book is that a meeting is a group activity and as such it belongs to the Chair *and* the members. The Chair may have particular duties – the main one being to keep the meeting under control – but the responsibility to ensure that the meeting achieves its purpose falls on everyone. The animated, vigorous give and take between the Chair and the members, and the cut and thrust between the members is what makes the meeting such an effective solver of problems and maker of decisions.

Meetings should also be rewarding for everyone involved. It is true that badly organised, badly run meetings are a bore to sit through and a terrible waste of time and money; but with a skilful Chair and well-motivated members, they should together achieve what they set out to do. That sense of achievement, apart from the practical results, is what makes meetings worth while.

PART ONE

1 Why have meetings?

Reasons for having meetings

Modern management shuns the compulsory meeting commandeered by a dictatorial boss who uses it to deliver a lecture or to push through his or her ideas. Modern managers are too intelligent, too highly trained, too independent and, it must be said, too expensive to waste in this way.

Meetings should be enjoyable. They should never be drudgery. People should go to them because they want to, not under duress, or out of a sense of duty. They should feel that they personally as well as their organisation will benefit from them, and they should come away knowing that they have spent their time usefully.

Of course not all meetings will be successful, not all will realise their potential or fulfil their purpose, and this can be for a number of causes, which we will go into; but the fact that many meetings do fail is no reason why the institution should be attacked or treated by those that use it as a necessary evil. Meetings are essential to modern management. They help:

- To bring people together
- To aid communications
- To inspire
- To energise
- To pool resources
- To liberate
- To get you noticed

Checklist

Good reasons for having meetings

☐ To bring people together

☐ To aid communications

☐ To inspire

☐ To energise

☐ To pool resources

☐ To liberate

☐ To get you noticed

☐ Meetings are natural

Bad reasons for having meetings

☐ To avoid responsibility

☐ To display power

☐ Out of habit

☐ To avoid work

☐ To avoid writing

☐ To rubberstamp decisions

Let us consider each one in turn.

■ *Meetings bring people together*

At first glance, this may seem an obvious statement but that makes it no less true or important. As organisations grow in size, so it becomes increasingly difficult for members to get to know one another, to plan and share ideas, and to follow the progress of those ideas. On the one hand, if you feel you are merely one small cog in a vast machine you are not likely to enjoy your working life, nor are you likely to give your most to that machine. On the other, the more you feel you are being recognised for the contribution you make to the organisation the more you are going to enjoy working for it.

This is where meetings help, because they bring a sense of cohesion and belonging to the members. No longer do they feel cut off from the way the machine operates; rather, they are an intimate part of that operation. This leads to greater job satisfaction which, in turn, leads to greater productivity – up to 25 per cent according to one survey. So everyone wins.

■ *Meetings aid communications*

The more people feel they are an integral part of their company or organisation, the happier and more fulfilled they are.

Communication is a vital part of this. Never being told what your management is thinking, planning, deciding about you, your work, or your future leads to a sense of isolation and this creates fear and with fear comes disaffection. It is very difficult, if not impossible, to give full attention and energy to your job if you don't know from day to day why you are doing it, what is expected of you, and what those who manage you think of you.

Meetings, short but to the point, regularly held between the head of a department, say, and the members of that department, can easily help to overcome that problem.

What happens to the individual within an organisation where there is lack of communication, namely, the growth of isolation and alienation, can happen also to groups within that organisation. They, too, can feel themselves cut off from the rest. In order that everyone involved has the opportunity to see something of the larger picture, it is vital for meetings to be held regularly between departments as well as between different levels of management. As a way of 'keeping in touch', especially when this involves more than two people, there is nothing to beat a meeting. If properly run, meetings can bring individuals together into a group and create for each member this inner sense of well-being.

A recent example of how useful meetings can be was told to me by a colleague who worked in a department in an international company which was, without reference to the people in it, sold off to another company. As a result, they all suddenly found themselves part of a new company which the parent company had taken over. Because they were all highly motivated individuals they objected to the way their lives and futures had been disposed of without consultation, so they left en masse and started their own company. Their employers deserved it, but one cannot help thinking that all the upheaval that affected everyone could have been avoided with a couple of meetings.

■ *Meetings inspire*
This is what the Managing Director of a large company described to me as 'Rah! Rah! Rah!' meetings, the ones that are called to fill a group with a new or a renewed sense of purpose.

All of us, no matter who we are, gain status from feeling part of an in-group. It starts in our childhood and remains with us throughout our lives. Membership of a group gives us a sense of identification, and when we are with the group we feel somehow stronger, more confident, more relaxed. We feel we can undertake tasks which on our own we would hesitate to tackle.

Meetings are an essential part of team building. The creating and sharing of the team goals, the exchange of expertise, the resolving of team conflicts and finally the satisfaction of seeing the goals achieved are experienced mainly through regular meetings of the team. Even when the team seems to be failing in its purpose, with the right person in the chair a meeting can turn defeat into victory.

■ *Meetings energise*
It has been said that groups are less creative than the individuals who form them, and that for solving problems, for instance, you need to have people doing their thinking on their own. While this may be true, the group is probably better at making final decisions than the individual.

Groups, especially democratic groups, where everyone has the chance to be heard and where the vote is free have the confidence to come to decisions that individuals might find too hard to take. Some say this is because no one single individual has to assume the responsibility of making the final decision or of suffering the consequences alone if the decision is wrong, and that, as a result, dangerous risks may be taken which the more cautious individual would avoid. But then sometimes, in business particularly, risks have to be taken. A good Chair, however, if aware of the danger, can always ensure that decisions are made only after careful deliberation and full discussion.

■ *Meetings pool resources*

As organisations grow more complex they also become more dispersed, with individuals and sections often situated in different towns or even countries. Information technology allows an increasing number of people to work on their own and to communicate mainly through the technology. There is the danger that, without the occasional meeting to monitor the progress of projects, time and resources can be wasted. Two or more people, for instance, may be struggling over the same problem without realising it. Meetings are the ideal venue for bringing expertise together, for charting progress, and for bringing up to date those who may have missed vital steps along the way.

■ *Meetings liberate*

A grievance aired is a grievance shared. Even in the best-run organisations, people get fed up, resentment develops against others or against the way certain procedures are carried out. If nothing is done about these grievances, they build up; work and productivity eventually suffer. Meetings allow those with grievances to air them freely in a safe and orderly environment. Whoever chairs such a meeting has their work cut out to ensure that the aggrieved get a fair hearing while seeing to it that the meeting does not get out of hand. The Chair, and the others at the meeting, will be given the chance to listen to the grievance, to understand the reasons for it, that the person who brought it to the meeting was not merely a 'troublemaker', and that, together, they will be able to find ways of dealing with it. The end result should be a much more contented and useful member of the workforce.

■ *Meetings get you noticed*

So far, I've been talking about how useful meetings are to organisations as a whole. Now a few words about how meetings can help you, personally. Being noticed in a company with a large workforce can be very difficult. The chances to shine in the normal working day do not come easily; but there is one place where you can make your mark and that is at the meeting. It does not really matter what kind of meeting, though it is probably easier to get noticed in smaller meetings with people you know and feel more at ease with than in large, formal meetings where you may be one of many strangers.

Much depends on how you approach the meeting and how you prepare for it. Before you get the wrong idea, I do not mean that you go in determined to shout louder than anyone else or to make a nuisance of yourself. That might get you noticed all right, but not in the way you would wish. No, I mean making an active and useful contribution to the meeting, which can be done in a quiet, yet forceful, manner.

If you are running your own meetings, your reputation as an effective Chair will stand you in good stead in other areas as well, because the skills required for the good handling of a meeting go to the very root of effective management. (For more useful advice on this see Chapter 9, on the role of the members.)

Finally, and perhaps most important,

■ *Meetings are natural*

Another obvious statement, perhaps, but it is a fact that human beings enjoy meeting other human beings, and for a very wide range of purposes. The warmth and friendliness generated through meeting is vital to our well-being as a species. The business meeting is, therefore, merely an extension of a very human characteristic. That it so often does not produce the same sense of satisfaction as the social meeting is not, I think, due to the nature of the meeting itself so much as to the way it is conducted.

The more formal the meeting, the more organised it has to be, but this should not necessarily spoil it for those who have to attend. A good business meeting should, theoretically, give to the Chair and the members a sense of satisfaction equal if different from that gained from the social meeting.

Reasons for not having meetings

If all the positive points that have been made above are true, why is it that so many people still think about meetings so negatively? Is it that many of the meetings they attend are unnecessary? This is more than likely, because, as we shall see, for almost every *good* reason for holding a meeting there is a *bad* one.

- Meeting to avoid responsibility
- Meeting to display power
- Meeting out of habit
- Meeting to avoid work
- Meeting to avoid writing
- Meeting to rubberstamp decisions

■ *Meeting to avoid responsibility*

Making decisions and taking responsibility for them is what being a manager is all about. Some managers prefer, if possible, not to take too many decisions on their own, so they call meetings. In this way they can spread the responsibility and if a decision is the wrong one, they can blame the meeting rather than themselves.

What may also occur is what has been identified as the 'risky shift' phenomenon whereby the meeting goes for the more radical rather than the more sensible decision because no one member feels individually responsible. (More of this later.)

When a problem arises, if the automatic response of a manager is, 'let's have a meeting' before other speedier, more decisive, and cheaper forms of action have been considered, then this should be a signal that the inability of that manager to take decisions and act upon them may be more significant than the problem itself.

■ *Meeting to display power*

The very act of calling a meeting is a declaration of power. Making everyone give up time to spend it at a meeting which you have brought together is making an unequivocal statement that you have the power over those who come to the meeting.

Regrettably, many meetings are called for that reason and no other though, of course, a more acceptable excuse is always given. Such meetings usually end up as monologues delivered by the Chair to a captive audience. Some information may be passed to the members, but most of it is unimportant or irrelevant to their jobs, and all of it is directed towards the greater glory of the leader.

▪ Meeting out of habit

'We always have a meeting on the first Friday of the month' is possibly the feeblest reason for holding a meeting. The original purpose might once have been a good one, but it has been lost in the dim, distant past. Once a meeting day, a meeting time and a meeting place are designated, people will create reasons for it, and spurious though these may be, they will allay everyone's suspicions that they are wasting their time. Quite likely the person who instigated the original meeting has left the organisation, so now no one can actually recall why it is held, but, because it has become somehow hallowed with time, no one has the courage to put a stop to it.

▪ Meeting to avoid work

No one will deny that sitting around chatting to colleagues about matters of mutual interest can be fun and no one's workday should be wholly devoid of such 'breaks'. It can also be validly argued that 'breaks' like that are work because a lot of creative thinking can be done when people are at their ease rather than under pressure.

But it is also true that meetings are called as an excuse not to work, especially when work involves the kind of hard, solitary thinking that many find daunting. A meeting called in such circumstances will achieve nothing, but it will give the participants the sense of having accomplished something. And the longer the meeting continues, the greater this false sense of achievement – something every manager should be on guard against.

The American comedian, Woody Allen, caught the absurdity of this in his film, *Annie Hall*, where two guests at a party in Los Angeles are trying in vain to set up a meeting. Of another guest one says, 'Not only is he a great agent, but he really gives good meetings.' In the end, when they fail, the first man complains, 'all the good meetings are taken'.

Research has shown that committees do not always think as clearly or as imaginatively as individuals. Some years ago 'brainstorming' meetings were very much in vogue becuse it was thought that if you bring a group of people together with different skills and encourage them to come up with ideas, no matter how wild, they will produce something far more brilliant than any individual could do.

This is not necessarily the case. The individual scores over the group for generating ideas. Meetings, however, are often better at *evaluating* ideas formulated elsewhere than individuals on their own.

■ *Meeting to avoid writing*

Some managers dislike writing memos or letters to colleagues, either out of laziness or a sense of inadequacy, so they call meetings to impart information that more properly belongs on paper, and, as a result, waste their colleagues' valuable time. A telephone call can be quicker than a meeting and just as effective. Yet many of these managers are so imbued with its magical aura that they cannot think of communicating with others except in terms of a meeting. Meetings for them become the sole reason for their existence.

■ *Meeting to rubberstamp decisions*

To be effective, a meeting should be as democratic as possible. Full information should be given on all topics under consideration and all the members should be encouraged to speak freely on those matters that concern them. Decisions reached are therefore based on thorough consultation and full deliberation and should be agreeable to most, if not all, the members.

Alas, not every meeting fulfils this high ideal. All too often, meetings are called by senior managers merely to rubberstamp decisions made by other people in other places. Sometimes the members are deliberately given too little information or the information is given too soon before the meeting (sometimes at the meeting itself), to allow them to make proper decisions and they therefore follow the decision suggested by the Chair. Such meetings are more shamocracy than democracy and no one, least of all the members, are fooled by them. They leave them, not with a sense of achievement, but feeling cheated as indeed they have been.

2 Who goes to meetings? The Chair

■ *Do meetings need a Chair?*

Given that a meeting is, or should be, a democratic process whereby a group of informed, conscientious and motivated people come together in a particular place for a particular purpose, there ought to be no need for someone to be officially 'in charge'. Together, each making his or her own contribution, they ought to be able to fulfil their purpose without a leader to control them.

Formal meetings, such as the annual general meeting of a public company, are required by law to have Chairs. The method by which they are appointed and their duties are laid down by the company's internal regulations which are in its Articles of Association.

Most meetings, however, do not have a formal Chair. Everyone gathers voluntarily around a table in someone's office to talk about a subject, and when they have satisfactorily reached their conclusions they separate until the next time they meet.

Some meetings seem to thrive better without anyone being appointed to lead the discussion, especially the 'brainstorming' session where the group comes together to generate as many ideas as possible on a given topic. The discussion is free-flowing, and when a workable decision is reached the meeting is brought to an end.

Yet, between formal meetings, which are governed by strict rules of procedure, and informal get-togethers, a vast number of meetings occur every day which are led by a Chair. Why should this be? The answer is simple: meetings are groups in action, and groups perform better with a leader than without one. With a leader, the Chair, the meeting is much more likely to achieve the purpose for which it was called.

■ *Who becomes the Chair of a meeting?*

The Chair may be:

– chosen or appointed by the meeting itself. This occurs more often in small, informal meetings among equals where everyone agrees that a particular member should take the Chair. His or her expertise in the subject of the meeting may determine the choice.

– chosen or appointed outside the meeting. For official or semi-official meetings, the Chair may be appointed by someone who does not actually take part in the meeting, e.g. a government-appointed Chair.

– appointed because of status. The Chairman or Managing Director of a company, for instance, will probably run most board meetings by virtue of his or her position. Similarly, the General Secretary of a union will conduct the union's executive council meetings although some organisations also have a Chair whose duty it is to conduct formal meetings.

– appointed by a senior member of the group. This is less common but it is a sign of confidence for a superior to appoint a subordinate to chair meetings, confidence both in himself and in the subordinate. Though it is not often done, it can be useful if the boss wishes to express his or her own view on a subject at the meeting, or to train someone to take his or her place at future meetings.

– chosen or appointed because of seniority. The repository of a group's history, usually its oldest member, may be chosen to chair meetings that involve the group's past as well as its future because he or she is expected to have greater insight into the way in which the group works.

– the person who calls the meeting. Again, this applies more to the small, informal meeting. Ambitious managers sometimes use this ploy to gain an advantage over their colleagues because it gives them a chance to show their mettle. If that is the only reason for calling the meeting, it will probably be a waste of time for everyone else.

■ *Who makes a good Chair?*

Basically, there are three types of Chair: (1) the authoritarian, who conducts meetings like military drills and wonders why nothing very original is ever said or achieved in them; (2) the permissive, who lets the members run the meetings, and wonders why so many of them end in chaos; and (3) the majority, who are a little of both and who wonder why other people's meetings seem more effective than their own. This is because being an effective Chair does not come naturally. It requires certain skills, but the good news is that these skills can be learnt and they can be improved with practice.

Which category do you fall into?

What follows is a list of characteristics for the ideal Chair against which you can compare yourself and your own performance. As in everything in life, it helps to know yourself, and if the meetings you run are not working out as you would like them to, then perhaps it is time to change.

A good Chair should:

Be flexible
Flexibility means that you will know when you have to be firm with the members of the meeting to maintain control, and when you can ease up so that they do not feel that you are bullying them and forcing them to come to conclusions that go against their real wishes. Flexibility also enables you to handle very difficult members, knowing again when to let them have their say, and when to give them enough rope so that they can hang themselves (which is often the best way to discipline the unruly).

Be confident
Easy enough to say, much more difficult to achieve. There is a vicious circle at work here, because if you do not have confidence in yourself, you will most likely make a mess of things in your first attempt at chairing a meeting and this, in turn, will undermine what little confidence you may possess. The answer, then, is to break that circle. But how? I am tempted to say 'fake it', but it involves a lot more that that. The first rule of conducting meetings is: *the prepared Chair is the confident Chair*. The more clearly you have worked out an agenda and have sorted out, either in your mind or on paper, the way you intend to run the meeting, the better are your chances of appearing confident even if your knees are shaking under the table.

Confidence also comes in with the way you dress, the way you speak, the way you use your eyes, your facial gestures, and your body in the course of the meeting. (All these subjects will be dealt with in greater detail in Part Two.)

Be authoritative

Authoritativeness is allied to confidence but goes deeper. The Chair who knows more about the subject of the meeting than anyone else clearly has an advantage and this will give him or her the necessary authoritativeness. However, lacking expertise in a subject does not mean you cannot be authoritative, or that you cannot run a meeting effectively. Acknowledging the expertise of others, being open to suggestions, avoiding forcing members to accept your point of view, not praising yourself and even taking the blame when appropriate – all these give you the authoritativeness which will earn you the respect of the members and make the task of running the meeting much easier.

Be fairminded

Do not look upon meetings as war. It was Sir Winston Churchill who made the distinction between the two: rather jaw jaw, he said, than war war. If you consider meetings as a necessary process to go through in order to achieve a particular result and not as a chance to get the better of your opponent, you are more likely to make a good Chair. It is possible that you are not going to like everyone at the meeting, or agree with all the views expressed. You are not required to. All you are asked to do is to treat everyone equally and to give all the members a fair hearing. The good Chair should be able to invite and accept the views of all without favouritism.

Be a good listener

Chairs tend to dominate meetings. Surveys show that most of them speak for as much as 50 per cent of the time, and so the rest of the members between them only get in the remaining 50 per cent. The good Chair should aim to keep his or her own contribution to a minimum – not more than 25 per cent – and let the members maintain the momentum of the meeting. The Chair can best contribute by introducing items, by asking questions, and by summarising. Good listening also entails:

- Proper concentration, which means taking in information as well as *appearing* to do so. It also means hearing not only what is being said but also what is not being said – those vital spaces between or behind the words that sometimes say more than the words themselves.

- Objectivity, that is, listening not only to what you want to hear but also to what you may not wish to hear, what may, in fact, be directly opposed to your own views. When listening, you should try to hear the whole story not just the parts that fit in with your own point of view.

- Empathy: not everyone is articulate, or capable of marshalling difficult arguments and presenting them in an interesting, logical manner. In fact, very few people are. Most of us bumble through, half-finishing one thought before jumping on to the next. Some of us find it difficult even to utter one complete sentence without stammering. The Chair who tries to help the speaker by constantly butting in, only ends up making life twice as hard for the speaker as well as for everyone else. On the other hand, the listening Chair is the one who possesses empathy – the ability to put himself or herself in the position of the speaker, to know what the speaker is suffering. With empathy comes understanding and with understanding comes the necessary patience to let the speaker finish in their own good time.

Be self-disciplined
You can't expect discipline from others unless you are disciplined in yourself. Good Chairs reveal this self-discipline in the orderly, organised way they:

- Prepare themselves for the meeting
- Prepare the meeting-place
- Dress
- Present themselves
- Conduct the meeting
- Time each speaker, each topic and the meeting as a whole

Have a good sense of humour
No matter how awkward the moment or difficult the member, the Chair who possesses a sense of humour can usually handle the situation with aplomb. The ability to laugh, especially at yourself, is a great gift. Having said that, I have to add a word of warning: one person's humour may be another's insult. The remark made to lighten the situation, if wrongly interpreted, can have just the opposite effect. That is why personal remarks about members of the

meeting, no matter how innocently meant, should always be avoided. It is usually safe to make a joke against yourself, but never against others: they may interpret it, at worst, as an attack on them, at best, as a lapse in your objectivity. If, therefore, you do not honestly believe you have the appropriate lightness of touch, do not try too hard to develop it. It probably won't work anyway. What you should always avoid is learning jokes to slip in at the 'right' moment. They seldom come off, so instead of putting everyone at ease you end up causing everyone, including yourself, acute embarrassment.

While on the subject, remember always to avoid sarcasm and facetiousness even though the behaviour of some members may sometimes tempt you to counterattack in this way. Even though you may succeed in controlling them, you have probably made enemies, or at least people who resent rather than respect you. Worse than that, instead of isolating them with your sharp tongue you may succeed in getting the others to sympathise with them.

Be familiar with the rules of procedure

Anyone who spends an hour or more a day chairing meetings should have a reasonable knowledge of the rules of procedure. If most of your meetings are informal, you will rarely be called upon to invoke these rules, but it is just as well to have them at your command in the event of problems or disputes. There are few things better calculated to put argumentative members in their place than a reference to *Citrine's ABC of Chairmanship*, or *Roberts' Rules of Order*. These books are both readily available and should be in the library of every manager.

Enjoy being a Chair

Chairing meetings should not be looked upon as a burden or an imposition but a chance to enjoy yourself. If the Chair arrives at a meeting with the attitude that it is an annoying interruption in the day's work, the members will very quickly pick up and adopt this attitude so that the meeting is doomed to fail right from the start. No one is saying that running meetings is easy. It is a challenge, but few events are more satisfying than organising and carrying one through effectively, seeing the disparate views and opinions, the attacks and challenges, the disagreements and dissensions all coming together in agreement. When this happens, you are justified in feeling pleased with yourself. The wrong attitude can become

Checklist

The characteristics of the ideal Chair

The ideal Chair should have:

☐ Flexibility

☐ Confidence

☐ Authoritativeness

☐ Fairmindedness

☐ Ability to listen

☐ Self-discipline

☐ A good sense of humour

☐ Familiarity with rules of procedure

☐ Fun being a Chair

self-defeating; the right one develops confidence and the result is a better Chair running better meetings.

The above list is not designed to cause you too much heart-searching. It is there for you to compare yourself against the whole range of qualities the ideal Chair should possess. None of us is perfect and it is our very imperfections that make us essentially what we are. Nevertheless I believe that if we feel we are not getting the best out of the committees and meetings we chair, then we should examine the list to see in what ways we may improve our performance. Only by overcoming our weaknesses can we build on our strengths.

Following from this, here is a checklist of how to be effective as a Chair.

■ *How to be an effective Chair*

Present yourself effectively

Show by your positive attitude that you intend to get the most out of the meeting. This will encourage the members to use the meeting to the full.

Be in control

Let everyone know by the confident way you take charge that you mean to carry out your agenda. Though you are not a teacher, your role is in some small degree similar, and every teacher knows that the first few minutes in front of a new class are the most important.

Be visible

Do not let the members take over the meeting, otherwise you become invisible and you might as well leave.

Be alert

Be aware of what is happening but at the same time think ahead so that you anticipate problems and are ready to meet them.

Be a good listener

Let the members do the talking. Remember, meetings are not excuses for harangues or for exhibitions.

Be humble

Unless you are the only expert present who has information to impart (in which case why not just a send a report or a memo instead of wasting everyone's time?), encourage the members to contribute their own expertise. No matter how subordinate they may be, if they feel you are interested to learn from them, you will get a lot more than if you ride roughshod over them. They may surprise you with information you are not even aware of. Your humility, genuine not false, also gives everyone a chance to shine, and through your meetings you may find the stars of the future.

Encourage fair play

It is not enough to be fair-minded yourself, you have to encourage this in the members too. If they see that you treat everyone equally and, just as important, you defend the weak against the strong, those tempted to bully will be forced by group pressure to fall into line. Be open-minded, ready to listen to all points of view, but don't allow factions and conspiracies to gain the upper hand.

Be unafraid

Frightened Chairs are ineffectual Chairs. If you are frightened of your members, you will not be able to control them; and if you are so worried about not making mistakes, or making the right impression, your attention will be distracted and you will not be able to run the meeting properly. Mistakes happen, no one can be expected to be on form every time, and not every meeting you chair will be a brilliant success. So what? Members are usually far more forgiving than you expect and anyway they do not go into every meeting with your own high expectations. So, if things go wrong, forgive yourself. It is much easier to put mistakes behind you if you do, and the next time, having learnt from experience, you can improve your performance.

Be yourself

Difficult though this may be, it is important to accept our own faults and learn to live with them. Where they can be altered then an effort should be made, but no one is expected to be perfect. Chairs who are at ease with themselves are much easier to be with. Members enjoy their meetings, and more work is done if the atmosphere is relaxed than if everyone is tense and anxious because the Chair is trying too hard to fill the role perfectly. If you feel this is happening to you then, as a first step, stop taking yourself too seriously. The ability to laugh at yourself is a great help. Try it.

Checklist

How to be effective as a Chair

☐   Present yourself effectively

☐   Be in control

☐   Be visible

☐   Be alert

☐   Be a good listener

☐   Be humble

☐   Encourage fair play

☐   Be unafraid

☐   Be yourself

3 Who Goes to meetings? The members

■ *Reasons for going to a meeting*

At any meeting, you will usually find members who:

- Have to be there because of their position in the organisation
- Have an interest, direct or indirect, in the result of the meeting
- Are expected or required to make a contribution (e.g. technical experts)
- Have been invited out of courtesy
- Are there because the Chair is trying to impress or find favour with them

In other words, just because a group of people get together for what ostensibly is a common purpose it does not mean that they either share that purpose or that, if they do, they are equally concerned in seeing that purpose achieved.

We have all at one time or another belonged to a group and so we know that groups behave differently from individuals. Meetings are groups in action and the people who go to them all bring to the meeting their own personalities, but once there another personality takes over – the group personality – and results can occur that none of the individuals thought likely or possible.

Group psychology has been well documented. I do not have the space to go into it in great detail here, but it is a fascinating subject which those who have to work with or in groups should spend a little time studying. Before we glance superficially at how groups work in the meeting context, let us examine the personalities you are likely to find in them at a meeting.

Some writers divide members into the good and the bad. This is an oversimplification, because the type of personality that may be bad in one meeting is ideal in another. For example, the member who always asks awkward questions will probably get on everyone's nerves in a meeting which is trying hard to reach an agreement on a difficult and divisive subject. But in another, more submissive meeting where the Chair dominates and everyone else lets things through 'on the nod', the awkward questioner may be making a very useful contribution. Also, we are all made up of many characteristics, and different circumstances bring out different aspects of our personalities.

Nonetheless, we can make some general observations about the *types* you may find yourself either sitting opposite or chairing at your next meeting. I have divided them into those who, in general, are **welcomed** at meetings and those who cause problems and are generally **unwelcomed**. And, as they say, to recognise them is to know them though not necessarily to love them.

■ *Welcomed Members*

The movers

Rule: Meetings need active members. Even if the Chair is doing a good job, active members participate fully, make useful contributions when called upon to do so, and sometimes when not, and in a variety of ways help to keep the meeting lively and interesting. Wise Chairs identify active members right at the start and keep them under observation, because they convey through the way they look, act and speak how they think the meeting is going, when they think it is moving briskly and when it is not going fast enough. Through their occasional questions and summaries, they also help the Chair to keep to the agenda.

The directors

By this term I do not mean *company* directors. I use the word to describe the type of person. Directors are clear-thinking and, because they often have a sound knowledge of procedure, they know how meetings are supposed to work. Chairs have so much to do they sometimes lose track of what is happening. One member may propose a line of action; a second member may suggest another, as a result of which the first may amend her proposal and so may the second. Unfortunately this is sometimes the kind of muddle meetings get into. This is where the director comes in with recommendations on how the Chair can get out of the muddle. Directors are also useful if Chairs get caught up in heated arguments with members, because they can see the wood for the trees, they help to sort out the substance from the quarrel and get the meeting back on track. They also help to point the meeting in the right direction when it threatens to go off on a tangent. Directors who overstep the mark can become bossy, pushing the meeting where they want it to go, and it is a temptation they have to fight against.

The summarisers

A sub-species of the director, these are the quieter members of the meeting who keep their contributions to a minimum. But although they may not say much, they listen to everything that is going on and know when to come in and make themselves heard. Like directors, they have clear minds and can remember what everyone has said. Thus when the subject matter of the discussion has become so involved that members start to repeat themselves or become bogged down in irrelevancies, the summariser is there to outline what has been discussed so that the Chair can once again take command of the meeting. What makes summarisers so useful is that their contributions are usually brief and to the point: they can go straight to the meat of the discussion, leaving out all the surplus fat.

The harmonisers

Thank heavens for them! Without them many meetings would collapse in recriminations and anger with no agreement and nothing accomplished. Harmonisers emerge from the most unlikely sources. Like summarisers they sit quietly until discussions start becoming heated when they realise that the Chair has lost control and unless something is done quickly and firmly, the meeting is finished. Their contribution is part summary, part direction, as well as a good helping of common sense. Because they are cool-headed and objective, harmonisers do not antagonise either side but, by revealing to the warring parties in a calm and orderly way the shared common ground and the advantages of reaching agreement, they bring them together.

The sociables

Meetings should not be excuses for getting away from the desk, nor should they be sociable events; but I believe that sociable people are needed to help groups work effectively. I do not mean the 'glad-handers' with their loud talk and louder jokes who embarrass the sensitive and annoy the rest. I mean those who, with a genuine sense of camaraderie – a kind word to one member before the meeting starts, an interested enquiry to another during a break or afterwards – can change a meeting from a dull one to a lively one. Sociables are the oil that makes the machinery of the meeting operate smoothly. If all the members are deadly serious; if they are involved only in the subject matter under discussion and not, even to the slightest extent, in each other; if all they are concerned about is finishing so they can leave and get on to something else, then the meeting will be solemn, heavy-going and boring – the kind anyone with any sense would want to avoid. Solemnity is not even a guarantee of success. Genuine sociables, because they help to make people care about each other and what they are doing, are rare and should be cultivated by all wise Chairs.

So much for the welcomed; now for the unwelcomed, and not just by the Chair but by all the members of the meeting, since these people spoil it for everyone. You will note that, unfortunately, there are more of them than of the welcomed. This may have something to do with the way groups work. Though membership of a group, as we shall see, helps keep most individuals in check, it also has the contradictory effect of bringing the worst out in others.

■ ### The Unwelcomed

The talkers

Meetings are for talking. Talking is the only way they can accomplish their purpose. But talkers do not confine their contributions to appropriate moments; they talk all the time, as though silence embarrasses them. They jump in whenever no one else is talking, and if the Chair does not keep them under control, they will even try to talk over others. Talkers, when denied their chance, become whisperers who try to run their own meeting on the side. They will chatter away under their breath to a neighbour, who is often too embarrassed to shut them up.

The know-alls

A sub-species of the talker, their frequent contributions are greeted by inward groans because there isn't a subject on the agenda that they are not capable of discussing – and at length. Unfortunataly, because sometimes they do know what they are talking about – if you speak on everything, by the law of averages you must *sometimes* get it right – the Chair cannot always silence them until they have got started, by which time it is usually too late. As much of the work of a committee tends to be repeated, the danger is that long-standing members who start as directors turn into the dreaded know-alls simply because they have been around a long time, they know what has happened in the past and more junior members do not have sufficient information to counter their intrusive views. Dealing effectively with the know-alls, as with all the other unwelcomed, is essentially the Chair's task though, as we shall see later, members can also help keep them in check.

The silent

Less obvious than the talkers, the silent can have just as deleterious an effect on a meeting. By making no contribution at all, they make it easier for talkers, among other unwelcomed, to take over. They also make it very heavy going for everyone and their silent presence creates a pall of gloom. The conscientious Chair will spend a disproportionate time trying to get them to join in and as a result the meeting will go on longer than intended. If this isn't bad enough, the silent frequently combine their silence with facial expressions far more eloquent than words, indicating for all to see their negative reactions to the Chair or a particular speaker. This is both provocative and cowardly. Its purpose is to upset others in such a way that makes no commitment to change or improve the situation.

The supine

Similar to the silent, these people appear to have no opinions, no views of their own, and usually have nothing to say. What they want above all else is a quiet life. They dislike argument, regarding it as an unwelcome intrusion into what should be the smooth running of the meeting. They are terrified of being seen to be different from the other members and can be relied upon to follow the majority if it comes to a vote. In discussion, they are easily swayed by those who talk the loudest or the most.

The conspirators

These people come to the meeting with a conspiracy already organised to push through or to block an item, or they are able, very quickly, to create a conspiracy in the course of the meeting. Interestingly, these members also see conspiracy in every opposition to their plans. Chairs have to be alert to these potentially destructive members who work to what is known as a 'hidden agenda', namely, an agenda on a subliminal level and known only to those in the conspiracy. (Individual members can also follow 'hidden agendas'. See Chapter 10, on what can go wrong with meetings.)

The obsessives

Beware the obsessives! Given even the slightest chance, they will drive the Chair and the rest of the meeting to distraction. They are stirred to life by only one subject, but they come to every meeting with just that in mind, and if the Chair or the membership is not on top of things, they contrive to get it discussed whether or not it is on the agenda. They are driven people and it takes considerable effort to stop them. Then, just when it seems that they have tired of the one subject, they come up with a new one, and the whole dreary business starts again. The attitude of obsessives is underlined by the fact that in ancient Greece an individual obsessed with an issue was called *idiotis* which, of course, bears a striking resemblance to the English word *idiot*.

You have now met the types of individual both useful and destructive who habitually come to meetings. But I repeat what I said earlier, they are *types*. Individuals are made up of different characteristics and very few conform strictly to any of the above categories. Even the welcomed can, in certain circumstances, become unwelcomed. The Chair or another member may for some reason irritate them or they disapprove of the way in which the meeting is being conducted and suddenly Jekyll turns into Hyde! As a Chair, therefore, or as an ordinary member of a meeting, it is better to treat everyone as an individual. But if you are faced by someone who seems to fall into one of the unwelcomed categories, then to know them is to be on your guard against them.

■ How to be an effective member

Come prepared

This means studying the agenda, reading all the relevant papers in advance, and noting down those points you particularly want to contribute to in the meeting. Preparedness also involves working out what you want to say to avoid taking up unnecessary time.

Speak clearly, simply, authoritatively and to the point

Members who express themselves badly do no one a favour, least of all themselves. Ordinary people are not expected to be able to marshal their arguments with the skill of a politician, but they are expected to talk in a language which is intelligible to all. Everyone should be capable of speaking up so that they can be clearly heard. If members mumble or make rambling speeches that stray off the subject and are impossible to follow, they are quickly going to be marked down as unwelcome.

Be a good listener

Members are not required or expected to speak to every item on the agenda, only those where they can make a useful contribution. Members who, when they are not speaking, are thinking about what they are going to say next, are missing half the meeting. Listening is far more important because only in that way is it possible to absorb the discussion and, when the time comes to speak, to do so with authority.

Be tactful and polite

It is never necessary to be rude or offensive, and personal attacks on the members should always be avoided. Members make far more impact on their colleagues and on the Chair if they confine their arguments to issues rather than personalities and treat those they disagree with respectfully.

Be patient

Chairs of meetings usually have lots to cope with and they may unwittingly overlook members who want to speak. Patient members know that if they bide their time they will finally get their chance and be calm enough to handle it with aplomb when it comes. Impatient members, on the other hand, will have made a nuisance of themselves trying to get noticed, and by the time they get the chance, their overwrought emotions will spoil their contribution.

Be unafraid

When conflicts arise at meetings members often find it difficult to know which side to take. The easiest option is always to follow the majority, but if members do not express their true feelings they are being dishonest, not only to the group, but, more importantly, to themselves. Acquiescence is not a sign of independence of thought or of courage. Everyone likes to be liked, but there are times when it is more important to take risks and go against the majority. In the end that is the way in which members make their impact on the group.

Be supportive to the Chair

Members who go out of their way to curry favour with the Chair are not a particularly attractive sight. On the other hand, those who feel they must always attack the Chair are a disruptive element that can ultimately ruin a meeting. However, those who, without toadying, can usually be relied upon to show their support are much appreciated by the Chair and are vital if the meeting is going to reach consensus and a satisfactory conclusion.

Avoid using the meeting for purposes other than those on the agenda

The purpose of a meeting is that stated on the agenda or agreed upon by the members. Good members will abide by that and not seek to use it to follow their own 'hidden agenda', which may be to score points against an opponent, bring up old hostilities, turn the meeting into a platform for their own views, or merely to show off. There is a fine line between making a mark and making an exhibition. Good members know how to tread it.

Members bring their good characteristics as well as their bad into meetings, but once they become part of a group, their individual personalities are taken over and to a large extent replaced by another, distinct personality, that of the group itself. This personality acts in ways different from the individuals which comprise it. To understand how groups work see Chapter 7.

Checklist

How to be an effective member

☐ Come prepared to the meeting

☐ Speak clearly and to the point

☐ Be a good listener

☐ Be tactful and polite

☐ Be patient

☐ Be unafraid

☐ Be supportive to the Chair

☐ Do not misuse the meeting

4 Who goes to meetings? The secretary

Meetings are business, and rather difficult business at that. The idea that a meeting is a few people sitting around a table chatting is why so many meetings are a waste of time and money. Successful meetings, even informal ones, require some effort and thought. Most of this is the Chair's responsibility, but good Chairs delegate some of their tasks to a secretary.

The secretary to the Chair may be:

- The Chair's personal secretary
- One of the members appointed by the Chair
- One of the members appointed by the meeting
- Secretary by virtue of his or her status in the organisation, i.e. the Company Secretary

Except for formal meetings, where, as in the last case, the secretary is appointed by the constitution of the organisation, everyone who goes to a meeting could one day find themselves performing the role of the secretary. Everyone, therefore, ought to know:

- What makes a good secretary, and
- What the secretary's duties are

Checklist

What makes a good secretary?

☐ Intelligence and clear-thinking

☐ A good memory

☐ The ability to organise

☐ Enjoyment of meetings

☐ The right status

☐ A calm personality

☐ Friendliness

☐ The right skills

☐ Being a good listener

☐ Open-mindedness and fairness

☐ Being well informed

☐ Clairvoyance

■ *What makes a good secretary?*

Good secretaries should:

Be intelligent and clear-thinking

There is a myth that any idiot can be a secretary, but anyone who has ever had to act as one will confirm that to do the job properly demands intelligence. For one thing, there are so many different tasks to keep in mind; for another, because the Chair as well as the members rely so much on the secretary, he or she has to do a lot of their thinking for them before, during and after the meeting.

Have a good memory

Secretaries have to remember what has happened before the meeting, e.g. at a previous meeting, what happens at the meeting itself (aiding their memories by taking notes), and what has to be done after the meeting. They should also remember personal details about the members of the meeting in case the Chair requires them. Their memory of previous hostilities, conflicts and conspiracies can be very helpful, especially to a new Chair.

Be good at, and enjoy, organising

This is probably the single most important characteristic of the good secretary. Meetings, even informal ones, tend to be organised rather than spontaneous events which means that for secretaries there is much organising to do, as we shall see when we come to examine their duties. But it is also essential that the secretary carry out these tasks with enthusiasm and not as a chore. Secretaries who regard their organisational duties as a necessary evil tend to be resentful and unhelpful.

Enjoy meetings

Similarly, secretaries who go to meetings because they have to and not because they want to hinder rather than help the Chair. Everything for them becomes an effort and their churlish attitude can mar the atmosphere of the meeting.

Be of the right status

That is, neither too junior nor too senior, neither too remote from the Chair nor the people attending, nor too closely involved. If secretaries are too junior they may not have sufficient skills to do the onerous job properly. If they are too senior, they may not take the meeting seriously enough. If they are too closely involved in the subject matter of the meeting, they will find it difficult to remain objective. People who are very ambitious do not necessarily make good secretaries because instead of enjoying what they are doing, they tend to treat meetings as a springboard to a more senior appointment. They are therefore less inclined to respect the Chair or to play what they regard as an inferior role.

Have a calm personality

Meetings, as everyone will agree, can be very fraught occasions. Being the Chair can be very lonely, especially when faced by hostility. Secretaries who handle their duties calmly provide good support and make life very much easier for the Chair. On the contrary, those who are easily panicked are worse than no secretary at all.

Be friendly

Meetings are more enjoyable and successful if the secretary has a friendly relationship with all the members. But friendliness should never cross the boundaries into friendship with any individual member, as the secretary would then find it difficult to treat the other members equally and to maintain the necessary objectivity towards them. A secretary should never convey by word or gesture that one member is favoured, or disfavoured, over the others.

Have the right skills

These include the obvious secretarial skills such as taking notes speedily, whether in shorthand or not, and typing accurately; but they also include the ability to write well so that the minutes drawn from the notes express exactly what happened at the meeting in a way that is literate, readable and to the point. (See the next section, on the secretary's duties.)

Be a good listener

As we've seen, this characteristic is shared with the Chair and with the members, but for a different reason. Secretaries are not usually required to make any active contribution to the meeting, so most of their time is, or should be, spent listening to what is going on. They have to be ready to assist the Chair at any moment, to answer a question, to recall something that may have occurred at a previous meeting but was not recorded in the minutes, to explain a point and, in formal meetings when called upon to do so, to provide the Chair with the appropriate rule of procedure. If they allow their attention to wander, they will not be ready when required.

Be open-minded and fair

It seems odd at first glance that a secretary should have to share this all-important characteristic with the Chair since, in most cases, the secretary is not involved directly in the discussions. Yet, like the Chair, good secretaries need to display a willingness to treat all members equally and without favouritism. Sometimes, unwittingly or deliberately, secretaries allow personal prejudices to interfere with the way they record the proceedings and this can have serious consequences for the members involved.

Be well informed

Secretaries, to be fully effective, need to know something about the subjects under discussion. They should, if possible, have at their fingertips details of the history of the committee. In addition, they should feel comfortable with the formalities. For formal meetings they will also be expected to know the laws and regulations governing the conduct of meetings.

Be clairvoyant

Just a joke! However, secretaries can help the Chair by looking ahead and anticipating the needs of the members, from basic details such as who prefers tea to coffee, to facts and figures that members might decide they need at the meeting. Inevitably some members will fail to bring the documents the secretary sent them, so copies will have to be provided. Secretaries ought to have sufficient experience to know in advance where problems may arise and how to deal with them, because the more they can anticipate and provide for what may be required at the meeting, the more the Chair can give his or her full attention to the running of the meeting.

As can be seen, the job of secretary entails a good deal more than mere organising, and the ideal secretary is as rare as the ideal Chair. Being only human they both have failings. But in the ideal relationship between Chair and secretary, what the one lacks the other provides so that together they make an efficient team.

Secretaries, however, are not, nor should they regard themselves as, indispensable. The Chair is the leader and must be seen by the members to be the leader. If the Chair appears to rely too heavily on the secretary and is, in fact, incapable of running the meeting without the secretary, he or she will forfeit the members' respect. Old-fashioned though it may sound, secretaries should know their place but as that place is right beside the Chair, it is the next most important one in the meeting.

■ *What are the secretary's duties?*

For ease of reference these can be divided into duties before, during and after the meeting.

Before

Deciding with the Chair:

- Who is to attend the meeting
- Where the meeting is to take place
- When the meeting is to take place
- Helping in the planning and preparation of the meeting, which includes:
  - Sending *notice* of the meeting to the members
  - Preparing working *documents*, reports or papers for the meeting
  - Helping the Chair to draw up the *agenda*, and sending out the agenda and documents well in advance of the meeting

In addition, the secretary's duties may also involve:

- Arranging the meeting room
- Arranging any audio-visual equipment that may be required
- Arranging for refreshments

Already it is obvious that the secretary's duties are considerable but they become even more so when we look at the planning and preparation for the meeting in more detail. (Organising the meeting room will be dealt with separately in Chapter 5.)

Notice

Formal notices are usually only sent out for formal meetings. In certain circumstances, i.e, for the annual general meetings of companies, written notice is a legal requirement. In any event written notices are always preferable to oral ones because, in the event of a dispute, the secretary will have a written record to confirm that notice was sent.

They should contain:

- The name of the relevant committee, where appropriate
- The date
- The place
- The time of the meeting

When meetings are held at venues that may not be known to all the members or are difficult to get to, travel instructions with a map and details of available transport should form part of the notice. Experienced secretaries know that details like this help the Chair's standing with the members and can make a difference to their attitude to the Chair and to the way they conduct themselves at the meeting.

Even for informal meetings, notice of some kind is essential, and part of the secretary's job is to find out whether members are available. Members should be given as much advance warning as possible. A telephone call ten minutes before is insufficient, because even if members can alter arrangements to get there, they are not going to be very co-operative. Getting members to a meeting is important; getting them there in the right frame of mind is equally important.

Documents

The more formal the meeting, the more working documents will be required. These can include minutes of a previous meeting, financial reports, reports of other committees, and copies of correspondence. Much work may have to go into their preparation, and it is essential that any documents presented to the meeting are accurately typed and correct in substance. The secretary must ascertain not only what the Chair or the members will refer to in the course of the meeting, but also what they *might* need.

The agenda

Of all the documents prepared and sent to the members, the agenda is the most important. Formal agendas for formal meetings follow a conventional pattern and always include the following items:

- Time and place of the meeting
- Purpose of the meeting

- Apologies received from members who are not attending the meeting
- The read and agreed minutes of the previous meeting
- Matters arising out of those minutes
- Items setting out the main work of the meeting
- Motions relating to the above
- Reports from sub-committees
- Contributions from specially invited guests
- Any other business
- Time, date and place of next meeting

The standard items in formal agendas should not give secretaries great difficulty; if in doubt, they can follow previous agendas. What may cause problems is the order of the items which relate to the substance of the meeting and here the secretary's experience can be vital. This, and the uses of an agenda in an informal meeting, will be discussed in detail in Part Two.

The agenda and accompanying papers should go out together well in advance of the meeting. *Rule: The usefulness of documents at meetings is in direct proportion to the length of time the members have had to study them.* Members who have had plenty of time can come to the meeting prepared to discuss the documents in an informed and intelligent way. They also have an advantage over those who have not read them. Documents presented at the meeting are very unwelcome; reading them while the meeting is in progress is time-consuming and distracting.

During

The secretary's duties during the meeting are just as onerous as those preceding it. In general they are as follows:

- Being on hand to make sure that everything is in order for the meeting before the members arrive.
- Helping the members find their places, if necessary.
- Keeping a record of what happens. In formal meetings, secretaries are required to take notes because it is on these notes that the minutes are based. In informal meetings, where minutes are not usually required, secretaries will probably only make notes of the

decisions reached. Nonetheless, the secretary's accuracy is vital. If conflicts arise over what actually took place, these notes will be the sole written record. When discussions become heated or obscure, it is sometimes difficult for anyone to know exactly what has been agreed upon. In these circumstances, the secretary may have to ask the Chair for clarification so that the record will be accurate.

- Helping the Chair to work through the agenda. Where the Chair is fully in control of the meeting, the secretary will have little to do in this respect. However, because many people do not handle meetings well, efficient secretaries have their work cut out for them. Their skill lies in helping to move the meeting forward without appearing to do so, otherwise the Chair will lose the respect of the members. They will have information at the ready if needed. They will quietly chivvy a Chair who talks too much or allows any of the members to hold the floor for too long. They will also help the Chair to encourage silent members to make a contribution. They will keep an eye on the clock, and if there is a danger of running over time they will warn the Chair in advance. They are not allowed to interfere, yet it is an essential part of their job to make sure that the meeting's purpose is accomplished.

- Ensuring that audio-visual equipment is in place and working properly and that there is adequate back-up if anything should fail.

- Looking after members' general well-being. Secretaries should make sure that the meeting room is comfortable and has adequate heating and lighting (more of this later); that there are paper and pens; that, if smoking is permitted, there is an adequate number of ashtrays; that there is water or fruit juice and glasses within easy reach; and finally, if there are breaks in the meeting, that more substantial refreshments are provided.

After

The secretary's duties do not end with the meeting, there is still much to be done.

- For formal meetings writing up the minutes and checking them over with the Chair. Here the secretary's notes play a vital role.

- For informal meetings, making sure that a proper record of decisions is kept so that it can be referred to later if necessary.

- Sending out the minutes to all the members.

- Following up decisions made at the meeting. This involves helping the Chair to check that all necessary action undertaken by any of the members has been carried out. Telephone calls may have to be made or letters written to remind members what they are required to do. Similarly, if the Chair has undertaken to carry out certain duties the secretary must check that they have been done.

- Finally, if the meeting asked to see particular letters or documents, ensuring that these are circulated to members.

It can be seen that the job of secretary is a crucial one and the success of a meeting depends to a large extent on how well this job is carried out. This is not to say that the chair is excused from carrying out his or her duties since ultimately the meeting is the Chair's responsibility. Ideally, the two should be working toward the same goal: achievement of the purpose for which the meeting was called.

Not all meetings need secretaries; only those which require some planning, and preparation. Then, delegating tasks best suited to the skills and essential qualities of a secretary leaves the Chair free to concentrate on running the meeting effectively.

5 Where do meetings take place?

■ *The venue*

Meetings can take place practically anywhere: someone's office, the corridor outside, the lift, the company canteen, the car park, or even in the car itself. We have seen that one of the first responsibilities the secretary and the Chair share is deciding on the venue, but this, of course, presupposes that the secretary is involved in the decision.

Meetings often take place on the spur of the moment and busy managers do not have the time to choose and arrange the meeting place; for this reason many meetings fail. Particularly if the venue is unsuitable or has not been properly prepared in advance.

Wherever possible forethought and planning should be given to choosing the venue, or the time saved by not thinking ahead will be wasted in an unproductive meeting.

The help of a secretary in choosing the meeting place can be vital. She or he should have a list of venues and information on when these are available and how much they will cost. The Chair's choice depends on two considerations:

- The *size* of the meeting
- The *purpose* of the meeting

The two, as we shall see, are closely interrelated. Let us consider:

The size of the meeting

Many years ago there was an advertisement for a shaving cream with the copy line 'Not too little and not too much – but just right!' This rule applies equally to meetings: 'Not too small and not too large'. It is more difficult to establish what is 'just right'.

Small meetings may be defined as a gathering of up to five members, large meetings as ten or more.

The advantages of *small meetings* are:

- They are cohesive. Members feel part of a working group and, in return, feel freer and more confident to make a contribution
- Productivity is high. People tend to prefer working in small groups and because of this they work harder
- All members are visible. They have less chance to hide behind other members and hope they will not be noticed
- Absenteeism is low. Everyone knows everyone else so the absence of a member will be noticed
- Cliques and conspiracies are identifiable. In meetings of less than six, it is obvious if two or three of the members have formed a sub-group to disrupt the meeting or force through a decision

The disadvantages are:

- There is difficulty in deciding who will take the chair if all members are of equal status. Without a Chair, disagreements become arguments, discussion mere conversation. Either way, chaos ensues and no conclusions are reached. In a two-handed meeting one member may veto the other; similarly, in a four-hander if two are against two, agreement is impossible
- Even if agreement is reached, decisions may not be reliable. The fewer the members, the less the breadth of experience and expertise, which means that the chance of biased opinions instead of informed views carrying the vote is greater
- Small meetings can become social occasions. As there

are too few members to keep control over the progress of the meeting, its character can easily change from business to pleasure

Although large meetings also have their advantages and disadvantages, it will be seen that the latter outweigh the former. The advantages of *large meetings* (of ten or more members) are:

- Decisions are sound. The experience and expertise of the members who come from a wide range of backgrounds ensures that decisions are carefully weighed and based on knowledge rather than prejudice
- More control is exerted. The Chair's duties are clearly defined, formal procedures are laid down, and if properly carried out, the meeting will progress in an orderly fashion
- Group pressure is effective on those who are unruly, disruptive or who threaten to take over the meeting

The disadvantages are:

- Too many formalities are restrictive. Rules of procedure get in the way of free discussion and frighten less confident members into silence
- Greater control is needed. To keep a large group of people working through an agenda means that the Chair has to be firm and disciplined. This means less opportunity for an open exchange of views
- There is more opportunity to hide. It is difficult for the Chair to keep an eye on everyone in a large meeting, so members of the silent brigade, if determined enough, can become almost invisible. For them, as for the rest of the meeting, their presence is pointless
- Meetings within meetings take place. If they don't talk too loudly and disrupt proceedings, it is possible for a few members to start their own meeting on a different subject. Consequently their contribution to the main meeting is minimal
- Cliques form. The Chair of a large meeting has to be extra vigilant to identify them, to avoid the risk of the

meeting being spoilt; the energy exerted in handling them is energy wasted

- Absenteeism is prevalent. In large groups individuals tend not to be noticed as much as in small groups, and for this reason they feel that their presence is unimportant. Unless the meeting is of immediate personal interest to them, they stay away

■ *The ideal size*

So if fewer than five members is too small and more than ten too large, the ideal size of a meeting is somewhere between six and nine.

Meetings of that number are the most productive because people enjoy working in groups where they will be noticed. They are therefore more likely to attend, make useful contributions to the discussion, avoid cliques, and be less disruptive. Nor will the Chair have to exert unnecessary pressure to keep the meeting in check. Agreement is possible, and decisions based on contributions from a wide range of skills and knowledge will be sound.

The purpose of the meeting

The purpose of the meeting, like the size of the meeting, influences the Chair's choice of venue.

There are two main types of meetings: *informal* and *formal*.

In the past, formal meetings were more common but, as working environments have become more democratic, so the informal meeting has taken over and is on the way to becoming the single most important method by which management and staff deal with the day-to-day running of their organisations.

A brief word on formal meetings. They usually require more preparation than informal meetings and, because of what is involved, many companies prefer to use outside organisations to arrange them. The choice of venue must be considered in detail because formal meetings tend to:

- Be larger in number
- Be longer in duration
- Be more expensive
- Involve more staff, therefore more delegation

- Require more equipment
- Require more elaborate seating arrangements
- Require more extensive catering

Formal meetings, like informal meetings, may be held for a variety of purposes from, say, boards of directors meetings to annual general meetings. In general their scope tends to be narrower and limited by law or by the constitution of the organisation holding them.

Informal meetings are far more varied in scope and less restrictive. They take various forms from small impromptu meetings arranged on the spot to semi-formal periodic meetings, such as those held regularly between management and staff.

There are seven main reasons to hold informal meetings:

- Decision making
- Problem solving
- Information sharing
- Negotiating
- Presenting and selling
- Team building
- Teaching and training

In addition, there are three subsidiary reasons, which are usually incorporated into the main reasons:

- Motivating
- Policy making
- Communicating

Many meetings have a mixture of purposes. Most, for instance, involve some form of communication, but in addition there is a particular kind of communicating in decision making which differs from presenting and selling which, in turn, differs from teaching and training. Communicating will also be found in team building where the members of the team are required to inform the meeting of their activities so that everyone knows who is doing what and thereby has a better overall picture of the team's progress. Motivating is an essential part of teaching and training, and, of course, team

Checklist

The ideal venue

- ☐ A rectangular room
- ☐ With sufficient space to accommodate everyone in comfort
- ☐ Quiet
- ☐ Well lit
- ☐ Airy
- ☐ With good acoustics
- ☐ Free from interruptions
- ☐ Pleasantly decorated
- ☐ Available
- ☐ In easy communication with the outside world
- ☐ Conveniently situated
- ☐ Available at a reasonable cost
- ☐ Agreeable to everyone present

building, but not necessarily of decision making. Policy is made only in certain meetings, for example, decision making and problem solving meetings. (For more on types of meetings, see Chapter 7.)

The room

Once the Chair has decided on the purpose and size of the meeting, the next decision to make is where it will be held. The rules governing the choice of the room are:*Everything that encourages or increases group participation is GOOD. Everything that inhibits it is BAD.*

The ideal room should:

■ *Be of the right size and shape*

Large informal meetings require large spacious rooms; small meetings should be in small rooms. If twenty people are crammed into a room meant for half that number they are going to be very uncomfortable and it does not take long for discomfort to displace interest. A small number of people in a large room may not be physically uncomfortable, but they will soon begin to feel awkward, and possibly anxious too, as they become aware of the empty space around them and listen to their voices echoing back at them. The shape is also important. The ideal shape is rectangular so that everyone can see and be seen. Long, narrow rooms should always be avoided. At a recent annual general meeting I attended the room was long and narrow and divided by columns, which meant that those at the back felt as though they were attending a different meeting from those in front.

■ *Be quiet*

Nothing distracts a meeting more than noise, intermittent or persistent. Unfortunately, not everyone speaks in a loud, clear voice and it is very difficult to concentrate when there is an argument in progress outside the room or a mechanic is fixing the coffee machine. Apart from the obvious culprits such as traffic and background office noise – loud voices, ringing telephones, typewriters – there are the less obvious but no less distracting sounds to guard against, like the hum of the air-conditioning and the buzz of fluorescent lighting.

But it is also important that the room should not be *too* quiet. Complete silence, if that is possible, can be deadening – if you have ever sat alone in a recording studio, you will know what I mean. It also gives the members the sense of being cut off and isolated from the rest of the world which, rather than putting them at ease, will make them anxious. Ideally, then, the room should be in surroundings where it is possible to *control* the level of noise.

■ *Be well lit*

Whatever the type of meeting, starting it in the right mood is important for success. The members should feel positive towards the Chair, towards the outcome, and towards each other. A darkened room is depressing. It is difficult for members to work up any enthusiasm if they have to stare through the gloom to see each other properly. This also allows members to doze off without being noticed. The lighting should provide illumination, but should not be too bright. Windows should be protected by blinds to prevent glare.

■ *Be airy*

These days with efficient air-conditioning, there is no excuse for a room to be either too hot or too cold since both will cause problems. If too cold, members devote all their energies to keeping warm rather than concentrating on the meeting. If too hot, they fall asleep. Clean, fresh air is ideal. Unfortunately, in many modern air-conditioned buildings windows cannot be opened, so one has to rely on the internal circulation of air which, of course, may not be as healthy as we would wish. Outdoors is not the answer either; there are simply too many distractions. Whether or not smoking is permitted is up to the members, but it can cause fierce arguments which can take up half the meeting time. A decision should be made at the beginning and adhered to strictly. The Chair may impose a ban, but it is probably better to leave it to the members to decide, otherwise the smokers may feel discriminated against. At a recent meeting I attended only one person smoked, but as she was the most influential member there, her preference carried the vote. Not fair, perhaps, but that's life. If smoking is allowed, an extractor fan, preferably silent, is essential.

■ *Have good acoustics*

If you have attended meetings where you have had to strain to hear what people are saying, you know how annoying and distracting it is, and how, after a while, you stop listening. The fact is, the Chair cannot rely on everyone speaking clearly. Many people are too embarrassed, too timorous, or have not been trained, to speak in public (and to the self-conscious individual, the most informal meeting is still public). Bad acoustics exacerbate the problem, and unless microphones are provided for everybody, half of what is said is wasted. Worse, misunderstandings about what was actually said cause serious difficulties later on. The acoustics, then, should be such that everyone can be heard clearly without echo and without strain.

■ *Be free from interruption*

Meetings are either as important as any other business or there is no reason to hold them. If the meeting is going to be continually disrupted by telephone calls or by other people coming in, it is a waste of everyone's time. Uninterrupted concentration is essential and it is everyone's responsibility – the Chair's as well as the members – to ensure it. It is not unknown for some members to arrange for calls to be put through to them while the meeting is in progress, not because of an emergency but to attract attention to themselves. Offenders should be given a warning by the Chair, and if they persist they should be struck off the invitation list.

■ *Be pleasantly decorated*

Décor is very much a subjective matter. What is ornate to one person is beautiful to another. The best décor is the kind that is not noticed but provides a good and efficient working environment for everyone. Stripped panelling or busy wallpaper can be distracting because they dazzle the eyes and make it difficult for people to look at each other properly.

When choosing the room, the Chair should also have in mind five other practical considerations:

■ *Availability*

This may sound obvious, but so often the Chair or the secretary has assumed the room they want is available only to find on the day that it has already been booked. This is why it is preferable to plan meetings well in advance. I have also suggested that the secretary keep a record of venues with details of cost, quality and availability which, since they are always changing, should be kept up to date.

■ *Ease of communication*

Business people feel uncomfortable if they are cut off from the outside world, so if the meeting is being held away from the members' normal surroundings it should not be so remote from telephones, computers, fax machines and the like that they are unable to communicate with their offices if they have to. There should also be someone available who can operate the equipment properly.

■ *Ease of travel*

As already noted, the aim of the Chair should be to have the members arriving at the meeting in a positive frame of mind, and nothing destroys this as much as a difficult journey. The Chair and the secretary, therefore, when planning the meeting, should take the trouble to find a venue that *all* the members can reach without undue problems, otherwise some may be justified in complaining that they are being penalised for living further away from the meeting place than the rest. This is increasingly becoming the case now that organisations are operating from different parts of the country. An accurate map of the area and details of travel arrangements should always be provided.

■ *Cost*

For informal meetings this is not usually a consideration, as most take place in the company's offices. It becomes important only when rooms have to be booked outside the organisation. The larger the meeting, the more expensive the room, so if you want to keep costs down limit the number of people you invite.

■ *Etiquette*

Protocol may be involved in deciding where the meeting is to take place. The Chair may, for instance, think it polite to hold a meeting, not in his or her own office, but in that of a colleague whose influence is considered vital to its success. Where to hold negotiating meetings sometimes causes almost as much controversy as the subject of the negotiations. If possible, a venue neutral to all parties should be chosen.

Preparing the room

This is the joint responsibility of the secretary and the Chair, so both should try to arrive early enough to make sure that everything is ready for the meeting. The Chair should check that the room, as far as possible, conforms to the requirements already mentioned.

In addition, both should check the following:

• The table or other writing surfaces must stand firmly and be adequate for the needs of the members. A small point, perhaps, but it is very irritating for members to try to write on an unsteady surface. Members should be seated sufficiently far apart to have enough space for the documents they bring with them.

- Chairs should be comfortable and offer support for backs. Sitting in a hard, upright chair for an hour or two can be painful, and after a while, the members will start thinking more of their backsides than the meeting. However, chairs with deep upholstery should be avoided; if they are too comfortable, they are an invitation to doze.

- Writing materials must be provided. The Chair cannot assume that members will remember to bring paper and pens to make notes.

- Name plates should be on tables. These are optional and are needed only for larger meetings. For smaller meetings members can find their own places unless the Chair prefers to suggest where each member sits. For large meetings where the members may not know each other, it is now common to provide identification badges.

- *Rule: Talking groups quickly dry up.* The Chair should make sure they don't by providing jugs of water and/or fruit juice. Even if someone else is catering, the Chair or the secretary must make sure that the water is fresh and cool and that the glasses are spotlessly clean. Attention to detail reflects well on the Chair, the secretary, and on their company.

- Other refreshments such as sweets, chocolates and biscuits are fine for some, but consideration should be given to members who are dieting, and for their sake keep these to a minimum. Cigarettes should be made available only if it is agreeable to everyone that smoking is allowed.

- Ensure that visual aids are available if needed, that they work properly, and that there are enough conveniently sited power points.

■ *Visual aids*

This is a large subject and readers interested in learning more are recommended to read relevant books on presentation skills. I will deal briefly only with the kinds of visual aid that might be used in an informal meeting. These are:

- The white board or, less commonly now, the blackboard with, of course, pen or chalk. Though not generally found in meeting rooms these days unless the rooms are also used for training sessions, they are useful if speakers wish to make an unprepared point visually.

Speakers should use them only if their handwriting is clear and legible.

- Flipcharts. These can be either previously prepared or blank sheets to be written on during the presentation. As an active device – with the pages turned over to make each point – they hold the audience's attention. Speakers, however, should feel comfortable turning from flipchart to audience and back again without losing their place. A pointer is a useful accompaniment. Blank sheets should be inserted at various places in the presentation to permit speakers to talk about something that does not require visual illustration. This avoids the audience having to stare at material on the flipchart which is irrelevant to the subject the speaker is discussing.

- A slide projector with slides. These can be a vivid and attention-grabbing way of illustrating points. But presenters should make sure that the slides are in the right order and the right way up before giving the presentation. Those embarrassing silences, punctuated by muttered apologies while the slides are being reassembled, destroy continuity and are a good way of losing the audience's respect. As with flipcharts, presenters should also ensure that blank slides are inserted into the presentation. One of the main disadvantages of slides is that the lights have to be dimmed and, if the presentation is held after lunch, the audience may be tempted to doze off.

- Overhead projectors. These are easier and much less expensive to prepare and set up than slides, and they can be just as compelling. As with slides, they need a proper screen for clear images; using a blank white wall is never as satisfactory. Acetates should be legible, the artwork simple and sharply drawn, and not too much information should appear on each one otherwise they will confuse, not clarify.

- Television, VCR and cassette players. As long as the equipment is in good working order, video and audio material can be very useful in training. Producing original material, especially for television, is prohibitively expensive for all but the richest organisations, and is the job of professionals. Better a good book or manual than a badly produced training and/or information video.

- Microphones and lecterns. The former are needed only for large, formal meetings where speakers are invariably inaudible. Lecterns are also useful in large meetings where members have notes to speak from but no table on which to rest them. Small, informal meetings should be held around a table and in rooms sufficiently free of noise not to require the use of a microphone even for speakers with quiet voices.

Remember that these devices are only *aids*. They are not, nor should they be, ends in themselves. You should not come to rely too heavily on them to do your work for you, but regard them merely as tools to help you make your main points more effectively. If you use them to illustrate *everything* you say, major as well as minor points, you will dilute their effectiveness. It does not matter how striking a diagram or a graph is, it is only useful if it is properly explained by the speaker and incorporated into the overall presentation.

It is also worth ensuring before giving the presentation that everyone can see what you are showing. You don't want to have to rearrange the seating while the meeting is in progress if some of the members complain they cannot see (see below for seating arrangements).

Make sure there are easily accessible power points for an overhead or slide projector. If the power point is out of reach of your equipment you may need to reorganise the whole room. This is disrupting and distracting, and will earn you the meeting's censure.

Check that the particular visual aid you want is available, and that you have the meeting's approval to take up time with your presentation.

If possible, try to get in a rehearsal or two *before* the meeting so that you can familiarise yourself with the equipment. All the good the aids may do will be ruined if used badly. This is not a case of learning on the job, because you would be doing so before busy people who do not have time to waste.

Note for the ambitious: If you are keen to be noticed by your superiors, arrive at the meeting with well-thought-out and properly drawn up visual aids to accompany the points you intend to make. As you will probably be the only one to do this, you will convey the impression that you are a person to be watched. It is not a good idea to use this stratagem too often, otherwise you will get the reputation not of being keen but of being a show-off and a bore.

Seating the members

How and where you seat the members and yourself depends on two factors: place and space.

■ *Place*

It is not always possible to arrange the seating exactly as you would like. The shape of the room may not be ideal, but it is the only room available, and you may have the only table available. You must therefore make the best of what you have.

Large meetings naturally require large rooms. In some circumstances, such as the annual general meeting of a major public corporation, only a small theatre or hall will do. The boardrooms of large companies are also substantial places, specifically designed to hold meetings of thirty or more. They are equipped with air-conditioning, soundproofing, correct lighting, and all the latest in modern electronic wizardry including individual computer terminals which allow the members to communicate directly with the Chair as well as to record their vote on each issue.

For meetings small or large the rule about seating is: *See and be seen.* This applies particularly to those who have to control the meeting, because one of the ways in which they do this is through direct eye contact with the members. The more members you can see and the more you can be seen by the members during the meeting, the more control you will have. (For more on eye contact and body language, see Chapter 7.)

To get the most out of a meeting as the Chair therefore, you should give careful thought to the arrangement of the seating, which, like the room itself, depends to some extent on the size, the type of the meeting, and the relationship and disposition of the members to each other and to you. The choices available for small meetings are usually greater than for large, but no less important, and the success of your meeting may depend on your making the right choice.

Here are some examples of how this works:

- One-to-one meetings, as for negotiations, are generally conducted across a desk; but in my view this makes them more confrontational than they need to be. Where possible, the parties should sit on the same side of the desk, their chairs angled at about 60°, preferably with a low table between them where they can place notes, or cups of tea and coffee. Larger negotiations, such as between management and workforce, are traditionally conducted by teams seated opposite each other. Would a round table not be more effective in bringing about an agreement?

- Senior managers often like to call meetings in their own office where they are surrounded by the trappings of power and success. Their large desks act as a barrier between them and their subordinates. They have a place to write while everyone else has to scribble on pads resting on their knees. Their chair is usually larger, more substantial, and in some cases even higher than everyone else's. Not surprisingly, meetings conducted in such conditions do not encourage the free exchange of ideas, but then they are probably not meant to. More likely they are being used either to feed the egos of those who call them or to railroad through a decision that has already been made.

- For brainstorming sessions, a round table is the most effective. The objective of such meetings is to come up with as many ideas as possible in the time allotted. For this an easy, free, open atmosphere is desired where everyone is of equal importance and has equal say. Control by the Chair is minimal. The round table fulfils all these requirements, though some writers argue that circles are too intense and that in these circumstances semicircles create a better balance of control and creativity.

- For team building, the round table again seems to me the best suited, because it is more democratic. The Chair wants everyone to feel free to make suggestions and to contribute equally to the team's goal. The problem with long or rectangular tables is that they confer status on members. Where a member is sitting can indicate a special relationship to the Chair, i.e. those seated nearest are generally considered more important than those seated further away.

- In problem-solving meetings the rule is: *opponents on the same side, alliances opposite each other*. For this a long, rectangular table is best since opponents seated on the *same* side of the table cannot turn the meeting into a confrontation; and members of an unofficial alliance on *opposite* sides of the table cannot easily communicate with each other, thereby breaking the meeting up. If the Chair is in need of a supporter, it is a good idea to seat him or her at the other end of the table, where they will have direct eye contact and can bring the meeting around to the Chair's way of thinking.

Whatever seating strategies you use, remember that the more you can see and be seen by the members, the greater your control over the meeting.

■ *Space*

When arranging the seating, it is also important to remember that human beings are very conscious of their personal space and may become tense and anxious if they feel this is being invaded. Watch, for instance, two travellers in the Underground battling for the armrest. It is not simply that each wants to have somewhere to rest their arm; it is their way of marking out their territory, their personal space.

Though there are variations between different national groups – Latin Americans, for example, stand closer to each other in groups than, say, the English – in general all human beings have fairly strict rules about who can come physically close to them. The distances graduate from immediate proximity for close family to between 4 and 9 feet for strangers.

The consequences of this are important for the seating arrangements at a meeting. Members, no matter how well they know each other, should always be regarded, not as intimates, nor yet as strangers, but as social acquaintances, which means that they should be seated no closer to each other than 18 inches and preferably about an arm's length away. Any closer and even the placing by one member of a book or a pen in what the other regards as his personal space may cause friction that can escalate into outright hostility.

Unfortunately, it is not possible to accommodate everyone's needs for maximum personal space; rooms and tables are simply not large enough. Secretaries and Chairs, when arranging seating, should be aware that the closer the members sit to each other, the more chance there is of hostility building up, which ultimately will be directed towards the Chair as the person responsible for their discomfort.

6 When do meetings take place?

In deciding when to call a meeting, four important points must be considered. They are:

- The time of day
- Who is coming
- The length of the meeting
- How to call the meeting

Let us take each one in turn.

The time of day

Rule: Successful meetings are planned meetings. Planning includes giving consideration to the best time of day for the meeting to take place. Many managers like to call meetings on the spur of the moment and sometimes, as in emergencies, this is inevitable. Unfortunately, some do it merely to show off their power – that, by lifting the telephone, they can summons half a dozen busy people to their office in ten minutes, making them give up whatever else they may be doing.

Petty dictators like that are a menace not only to those who are subject to their whims but to the organisation as a whole, because their 'meetings' are no more than an excuse to give a lecture or make a speech, and, as such, are a waste of everyone's time.

Self-confident managers, who do not need to impress others, call meetings only when they think they are necessary, and they plan ahead.

Ideally, meetings should be arranged at a time when all the members are at their mental and physical peak, when they are most creative, energetic and decisive, but it is impossible to determine this for everyone. Some are morning people, ready to give their best the moment they enter the office; some only start to get into their stride by mid-morning; others peak in the early afternoon, and there are some who are at their best in the evening (a problem if you have a nine-to-five job!).

Even if the impossible happens, and all members are at their most dynamic at the same time, the chances that they will all be available are very slender. The availability of the room, if it is not the manager's own office, may also present a problem, so managers should call a meeting only after they have given thought to these points.

Leaving aside individual preferences, certain times of day are better and some are worse than others. Let us first look at those periods which, if possible, should either be avoided or chosen only when no other time is available.

- Immediately prior to lunch: for obvious reasons, this is not a desirable time because people's energies are usually low and their thoughts more on the meal they are hoping to have than on business.

- Meetings immediately after lunch can be very hard going, even if the lunch was just a sandwich, let alone a large meal served with alcohol. Concentrating on solving awkward problems, on making negotiating points or absorbing new information is never easy, but is made doubly difficult when members are seated in comfortable chairs in a warm room, trying to fight off sleep.

- Are lunchtime meetings a good idea? Those in favour take the view that for, say, negotiating, the congenial atmosphere, good food and possibly alcohol break down barriers, relax the negotiators, and put them in a positive frame of mind to reach a compromise. They also argue that meetings over lunch, despite the high price of a meal in a good restaurant, are cost-effective because people have to eat so they may as well work while they are eating.

Those who argue against lunchtime meetings say that it is very difficult to concentrate on important and complicated matters while trying at the same time to order food and eat it. Though it can be avoided, there is a temptation to drink, especially if someone else is paying for it, and even a little alcohol can impair judgement so that foolish or ill-considered decisions are more likely to be made than when meeting in an office. Some doctors argue that lunchtime meetings are unhealthy. People tend to eat rich, fatty food, high in cholesterol, and this, combined with the stress of talking business, is bad for the heart.

Irrespective of these arguments, managers will go on having lunchtime meetings if they are thought convenient.

- Breakfast meetings are common in the United States and, in spite of some initial resistance, have become increasingly popular on this side of the Atlantic. Enter any American hotel dining-room at any time from 7.00 a.m. onwards and you are bound to see tables of men and women in deep discussion while downing coffee, ham, eggs and pancakes.

The same arguments for and against lunchtime meetings, excepting the question of alcohol, apply to breakfast meetings and, as both are here to stay, it is important that they are organised and planned with the same care as meetings at any other time of the day.

Where they are held should be carefully considered. The restaurant should not be too noisy or too crowded, the service should be efficient but not too intrusive, and thought should be given to the food served from the point of view of health. To avoid the embarrassment of choosing the wrong place, managers should visit the restaurant before arranging the meeting; and since they will probably make the reservations, secretaries should have a list of the most suitable restaurants.

- The end of the day is not a good time for a meeting, especially if it is a Friday. Whatever type of meeting, the ability to concentrate on the agenda is vital, and if members are thinking about their journey home or what they are going to do at the weekend, they are much less likely to pay attention to what is going on at the meeting. Members will also be eager to reach agreement, whether or not it is in their best interests – which is precisely why crafty managers choose the last thing on a Friday to call a problematic meeting.

It is worth remembering that, no matter how unsuitable the time of day, or lacking in energy the members, strong motivation will overcome inconvenience, distractions – and even a good lunch. If the meeting is motivated to reach a consensus, solve a problem, or make a decision, it will do so. Responsibility for motivating the members lies with the Chair and how this is done depends on the Chair's personality, on how the meeting is planned and how it is run.

Who is coming

For most day-to-day meetings, where the majority of the members belong to the same department or are on similar management levels, the time when the meeting is held has little or nothing to do with who is being invited. But in certain circumstances the people the Chair wishes to invite will influence when the meeting is called.

■ *Top management*

The higher up in the hierarchy of the company managers are, the more meetings they attend and accordingly the more difficult it is to ensure their presence. It is not unusual for senior managers to be booked up, not days, nor even weeks, but months in advance. The Chair, therefore, must weigh up in good time the importance of the meeting against the importance of their presence. It may be that decisions cannot be reached without them in which case the meeting has to be arranged around their timetable; but it may be that their presence is desired simply to accord status to the meeting and, incidentally, to the Chair who managed to get them there, in which case the meeting should go on without them. It has been found that rather than helping members to reach a consensus, high-status individuals, because of their importance, can dominate the meeting and cow the members into accepting their point of view against the members' own interests.

■ *Experts*

Part of the Chair's skill is in choosing the right people for the meeting. If it is being called to reach a decision on, say, whether or not to install a new computer, who is the best person to ask: the technical expert whose knowledge is mainly theoretical or the one who will eventually work the computer? Naturally, when important decisions like that have to be made, the Chair will want to have those who know most about the subject otherwise it could prove very costly for the company. But who are they? Shortsighted managers will always pick the technical experts even if it means delaying the meeting to fit into their busy timetable rather than someone more accessible but of a lowlier status whose practical working knowledge could be vital.

■ *Guests*

Sometimes it is essential to the success of a meeting to invite special guests. They may be technical people, or those with a particular talent, as, for instance, when a brainstorming group working on promoting their organisation bring in an illustrator to visualise some of their ideas. A guest from one organisation may be invited to attend a meeting in another as liaison between the two. The Chair has to decide how essential the guest's presence is and whether or not it is worth postponing a meeting to fit into his or her busy schedule. Chairs, however, should guard against the temptation to invite someone well-known merely to give their meeting more status if doing so outweighs more practical considerations, like the convenience of everyone else.

Chairs must remember that before deciding who to invite to the meeting, they must decide what its purpose is. Whether or not a meeting is successful depends, not on how many eminent people attended, but on whether or not it achieved its objectives. In fact, experienced Chairs have found that a predominance of highly talented members does not necessarily ensure that the best decisions are made. Decisions made by those on a lower level are very often more responsible and mature.

Another note of warning: It is not always a good idea to have too much of a mixture of members at the meeting, i.e. managers from various levels of management, or specialists from different disciplines. Good meetings, as with all effective group activities, depend on the members sharing some common ground, and if that is missing then it is too easy for the meeting to dissolve into arguments about status and position. A mixed meeting is just like a cocktail with too many ingredients: the experience while it lasts may be stimulating, but the result is a nasty headache.

The length of the meeting

Rule One: the larger the meeting, the longer it will last.

Rule Two: longer does not mean better.

Anyone who has ever sat on a committee must have experienced the meeting without an end. The unrelieved tedium of listening to members arguing at great length over insignificant items or making long, boring speeches on matters of interest only to themselves; of watching the Chair struggling to keep to the agenda and failing; and of praying for a decision to be reached so that everyone can go home – this is the nearest to Hell on earth that most of us are ever likely to come.

It has been calculated that what can be decided by four people in twenty minutes takes eight people *five* hours! It has also been calculated that the average concentration span is between 60 and 90 minutes. Yet this does not stop lots of people in companies and organisations all over the country from packing into small rooms for long hours of talk. The exercise is wasteful in time, money and human resources.

Yet Chairs are responsible for making sure that their meetings achieve their objectives, even if it takes time. So they have to perform a difficult balancing act: keeping a close eye on the time while giving everyone a chance to contribute to the discussion so that agreement is finally reached.

Here are some hints on how to do this:

- Start at the planning stage by drawing up an agenda before the meeting.

- Encourage your members to think ahead about the subject of the meeting. This way, they will come better prepared to discuss it in an informed and competent manner.

- Set a time limit for the meeting as a whole as well as for each item on the agenda.

- Tell the members at the start of the meeting how long the meeting will last. By getting them to agree, it becomes a team goal to bring the meeting to an end in time.

- Stick to your agenda. The problem of the never-ending meeting is largely a control problem. By keeping to the agenda, you can reach your objective in the time allotted without sacrificing proper debate.

- Go for a majority decision rather than unanimous agreement even though it might mean a follow-up meeting, because the minority still need to be convinced. But if, to achieve unanimity, your meeting has to go on for hours, you would be best advised to get what you can and call it a day.

- *Rule: when acquaintances get together, they prefer to gossip than to work.* As the Chair, be vigilant. Cut out the chat. Get the members to concentrate on the agenda by making it as interesting and involving as possible for them.

- Build in breaks. If the meeting looks as if it is going to last for longer than an hour and a half, arrange to have refreshments served. Some writers suggest that, to save time, these should be brought to the table so that the meeting can continue while people drink their tea or coffee. I think it is better if the members get a chance to stretch their legs. Their batteries will be recharged and when they sit down again they will be ready to push through to the end.

- Make your meetings enjoyable: a tall order but not impossible. When chairing a meeting you have to take the proceedings seriously, but that does not mean you have to take *yourself* seriously. An ability to laugh, especially at yourself, helps to lighten the atmosphere and makes everyone more relaxed so that the meeting can achieve its purpose with the minimum of tension and hostility.

When setting a time limit for the meeting, you have to go back to basics and ask yourself:

- Why are we meeting?
- How difficult is our job?
- Can the people I've invited cope?

Though you as the Chair are primarily responsible for answering these questions, you are not alone. Meetings are a group activity – since we no longer hunt game for food, probably our most common group activity – so the answers must also come from the members. Together you will bring focus to the business of the meeting, together you will decide how complex that business is, and together you will decide whether you have the skills to deal with it.

Everyone gains if the meeting reaches a satisfactory conclusion in good time and everyone suffers if it does not, so it is in the interest of all to agree on the reason for the meeting, and to limit the meeting to what you can comfortably handle.

Checklist

Calling the meeting

Chair

☐ Check diaries

☐ Telephone or send written notice

☐ Send agenda and accompanying documents

Members

☐ Note details of meeting

☐ Notify non-attendance

☐ Arrange travel

How to call the meeting

In the previous chapter we saw that, although Chairs frequently leave the arranging and calling of meetings to their secretaries, the ultimate responsibility for the correct carrying out of the procedure remains with the Chair. Here, then, is a checklist.

■ *Check diaries*

Make sure that the date proposed for the meeting is free. This seems elementary advice, yet it is just as well to mention it because Chairs or their secretaries quite often double-book dates. Some, it has to be said, do it deliberately to impress their colleagues with how busy they are, but I think we can assume that they are the exceptions and that most would find it awkward to have to cancel a meeting because of one previously arranged.

■ *Telephone or send written notice*

This is just in case proof is later required by the Chair that due notice was given. For formal company meetings, giving proper notice is essential. If, for example, you have an extraordinary general meeting in the Outer Hebrides, which can only be reached by helicopter at midnight, the courts tend to think that is not proper notice. Proper notice must be reasonable in all circumstances; it has to be at a time and place when all those entitled to attend can reasonably do so. The amount of notice that must be given is laid down in the internal regulations of the company, which are its Articles of Association.

The notice ought to mention the following:
– Date of the meeting. Remember that busy people need to be told well in advance; you cannot expect them to drop everything just because you want them.
– Place of the meeting. Don't forget also to send detailed instructions how to get there, especially if your invitees are not familiar with the location of the venue. Worse than useless is a roughly drawn map with only some of the roads shown. What is needed is a photocopy of a good map with the meeting place clearly pointed out.
– Starting time of the meeting. It is a good idea to add a request to invitees that they arrive a little beforehand to ensure that the meeting begins promptly. The promise of refreshments served on arrival could make the request more tempting.
– Finishing time of the meeting. Some Chairs do not like to be tied

down by this. The member's expectations are raised and they become impatient if it seems that the meeting will not end on time. This is precisely why I think it is a good idea: it avoids open-ended meetings.

■ *Send agenda and accompanying documents*

For informal, single-subject meetings, Chairs usually do not bother with written agendas. If, however, the meeting covers a number of subjects, an agenda makes keeping control easier. Their task will be further lightened if members know in advance exactly what the meeting is about and come prepared. If there are documents that they need to study, these should be sent with the notice.

Members, on receiving their notice, should:

■ *Note details of meeting*

Put the date, time and place of the meeting in their diary immediately, to avoid the embarrassment of double-booking. Keep the notice in a safe place in case it is required to gain entry to the meeting.

■ *Notify non-attendance*

Inform the Chair or the secretary if they cannot attend. Apart from being good manners, this helps the Chair to make the necessary arrangements for the room and for providing refreshments. Also, if too few members are able to attend, the meeting may have to be postponed. The Chair is entitled to assume that everyone invited will be attending unless he or she hears to the contrary.

■ *Arrange travel*

Work out travel arrangements in advance if the address of the meeting is unfamiliar. So often members wait till the last minute to find out where the meeting is then get lost in their rush to find the place. Arriving late disrupts the proceedings and can usually be avoided with a little forethought.

PART TWO

7 What happens at meetings?

Before we examine in what ways meetings differ, let us remind ourselves what they have in common.

Meetings occur when:

- Two or more people come together
- In the same place and at the same time
- For a purpose
- Which has been decided upon in advance
- Usually by one person, the Chair, who also controls it
- By the implied or express consent of the members
- According to past practice or specific rules

All these elements are necessary before a gathering of people can accurately be described as a meeting. Each element has important consequences and they are interdependent. Thus, the number of people invited by the Chair, and who they are, depends to some extent on the purpose. The membership and the purpose may affect where the meeting is held and how long it will take. Who sits in the Chair may be determined by the purpose or it may be governed by the rules of the meeting. The rules may, in turn, be governed by the purpose, and so on.

Meetings are groups in action and we should now look at how groups work.

■ *How groups work*

Groups are effective because they operate on the principle known as synergy, namely, the whole is greater than the sum of the parts. This means that the collective action of the group produces more than would be produced by the individuals making up the group; the collective memory of the group is greater than that of its members; and the group's sum of knowledge surpasses that of the individuals within it.

Individuals are good at creating ideas; groups are better at testing them, because the members can draw on a wider range of experience. For example, a manufacturing company wishes to expand, but is not sure in which direction to go. One of the directors suggests buying a retail shop in which to sell goods manufactured by the company. He has made enquiries and has found what he thinks is the ideal shop to purchase. Now, the idea has to be put to a meeting of fellow directors to decide whether or not to go ahead with the scheme. Present are the managing director, who has been running the company for twenty years and has a wealth of experience behind him, the finance director, the sales and the personnel director, each with their own areas of expertise. Together they are in a far better position to look at the scheme from various angles than any one of them acting alone.

Groups do not necessarily work harder than individuals, but they can work for longer. They can also be more easily distracted. How often have you sat in a meeting about one topic only to find that most of the time has been spent arguing about something else? Groups are not always as tenacious as individuals. They will sometimes go for the soft option instead of struggling against difficulties to reach a conclusion.

To function effectively, groups need direction. They must have goals which they not only know about but also share. These goals should be made clear to them from the start. For this reason it is vital that, at the beginning of the meeting, the Chair explains to the members what the meeting is for. Members can then focus their attention on that goal and work towards it.

Groups go through four stages of development:

In the first stage, the group comes together and the individuals establish a tentative relationship with each other. This generates a certain amount of anxiety and it is mainly up to the leader, i.e. the Chair, to strengthen the bonds between them by clearly establishing what kind of behaviour is acceptable and what is not.

In the second stage, conflicts arise within the group which have to be overcome if the group is to survive. Members may rebel against the Chair or turn on each other. Some will conform, others will resist pressures brought by the group to do so.

In the third stage, the group finds a common way of carrying out their task(s). Views and feelings are exchanged more openly, conflicts are smoothed over and a sense of mutual support develops.

In the final stage, the group is working towards its common goal. Problems are resolved and the group's energies are no longer spent in conflict but are directed towards realising the goal.
NB. The role of the leader (the Chair) is crucial in all these stages. The way in which he or she handles the group will directly affect its outcome.

In order to survive, a group resists deviation by putting pressure on those who challenge it. Firstly the group will try reason to make dissenters change. If that does not work, the group will try to apply emotional pressure, appealing to loyalty, patriotism and so on. Finally, and most effectively, the group will threaten to isolate the deviants and, if they still persist in their challenge, the group will apply the ultimate sanction and reject them.

Individuals conform to the group to avoid rejection, whether or not they accept the group's beliefs. After a while they 'internalise' these beliefs, which then become part of their own behaviour, and they will themselves turn on any deviants.

Groups tend to be conservative. They resist change and prevent their members from changing. However, because they share responsibility for decisions, they might also take risks that individuals would hesitate to take.

What happens when groups meet

Meetings are where groups do their collective business. The members meet as a group at an agreed time and place, appoint a Chair, who is usually but not always the leader. They also appoint members to other roles, such as secretary, treasurer, and so on; and they establish and agree on proper procedures for running their meetings. These may be written down in a constitution.

At the meetings discussions follow a pattern. A statement is made or a question asked by the leader (the Chair) and various members contribute their views, after which the Chair tries to obtain a consensus before moving on to the next subject. Though groups may be democratic there is still a tendency for the members with higher status to be given more time to speak and to be listened to with greater care than less important members.

Meetings help groups in the following ways:

- They provide a forum for discussion which makes it easier for those within the group to make contact, and to communicate with one another
- Though meetings are not essentially sociable occasions, they provide a mutually acceptable place for members to relate to each other on a regular, if impermanent, basis
- Meetings cement groups' collective identity. Common goals are established and regularly reinforced at meetings. Individuals come to identify with, and commit themselves to, those goals and cohere into the group
- After successful meetings members sense their collective strength and oneness which separate them from others who do not belong to the group. This powerful sense of 'them' and 'us' is important to the continuing survival of the group

By coming together in the same room at the same time to discuss topics of common interest, the 'me' is turned into the 'we'. Individual personalities merge into the group personality with an identity of its own, an identity, moreover, that is different from that of other groups.

As a way of running groups, meetings have both advantages and disadvantages.

On the plus side, meetings help to develop good relationships and maintain channels of communication between the members, thereby reinforcing a sense of commitment by each member to the group. It is also through meetings that one group can be linked to, and communicate with, other groups.

On the minus side, meetings are not always as democratic as they pretend to be, because some members are more equal than others. Those who the group consider are important get more time to express their ideas and these ideas are treated more seriously than the others. Groups also tend not to be as good at creating ideas as the individuals who form them, yet they may take riskier decisions than individuals acting on their own.

It is between these positive and negative limits that most meetings operate.

■ *Making use of non-verbal communication*

In meetings we speak with our voices. We also speak with our bodies, our eyes and our facial expressions. In fact, we give out five times more information with this non-verbal language than we do with ordinary language.

Sometimes when we say one thing, our bodies communicate the opposite. We may, for example, state that we agree to a proposal but our facial expressions indicate that we do not. In answer to your enquiry about someone's state of health, she may reply, 'Fine', but the way she stands, the dull look in her eyes, the tight lips, tell you far more clearly that she is feeling terrible.

Most of the gestures we make are automatic. They are our natural response to a particular situation. We do not usually think: I'm frowning, or, I'm tapping my fingers, and it is just as well we don't because then our gestures would become contrived and unnatural. But, since meetings are essentially about give and take, about the accurate expression and the equally accurate reception of information, it is important for anyone attending or running a meeting to be aware of what they are doing so as to know how to make non-verbal communication work for the individual's as well as for the meeting's benefit.

There are basically three separate but closely interconnected ways in which we communicate non-verbally: (1) Looking, (2) Behaving and (3) Listening.

Let us examine each one in turn.

Looking

Looking helps you control the meeting, which is why it is vital to remember when you set up the room that you can clearly see and be seen by everyone. You make eye contact with members to indicate that it is their turn to speak. Looking at them while they speak tells them that you are interested in what they have to say. Looking away at a critical moment may be saying that your interest has ceased, or that you do not approve of their contribution, and since it is your duty to remain as neutral as possible, it is a good idea to cultivate an expression that gives nothing away except continuing interest.

Looking sends out different messages. You look at one member when she has spoken long enough. You look at another to warn him that he is not giving the meeting his full attention, and you look at a third to caution her in advance against losing her temper.

Members, of course, also look at you in the chair and you can read from their expressions what they are thinking about the way you are handling the meeting. They may be telling you that you are talking too much and that time is moving on. They may tell you that the debate on a particular item has gone on for too long. They may also warn you that an argument is about to start unless you intervene. It will help you, therefore, to glance around the table every now and then to see how your efforts are being received.

Members who sit gazing fixedly at the ceiling or the opposite wall may be saying, 'I'm deep in thought and don't want to be disturbed', but more likely, 'I'm bored'. In some cases they may be saying, 'I'm superior to the rest of you and don't have to participate'. Those who seldom raise their heads and stare at the table in front of them signal nervousness and lack of confidence. As Chair, you should take appropriate measures to ensure that they are brought back into the centre of the meeting.

Members communicate with each other through eye contact, and as a member you ought to be aware of what your looks are saying to the others in case they give more away than you intend.

The best kind of looking is that which says, 'I am interested in, and concentrating on, everything that is going on', because this makes a positive contribution to the meeting, and the Chair will value you all the more for it.

Unlike the Chair, you are not obliged to remain neutral, but are free to signal your approval or disapproval of something said by another member. In the event of a disagreement, you can make your position clear to others by your expression. If, however, you want to keep your options open, then, like the Chair, you ought to maintain a neutral expression.

Mostly, being looked at is satisfying and enjoyable, but as we all know it can also be unpleasant. 'If looks can kill' may be an exaggeration, but if you gaze at another for too long you can make them feel threatened and anxious. Gazing at another member may also be sending out signals that you are interested in him or her not just as a member of the meeting but on a personal level, which can be embarrassing for them.

Used by the Chair at appropriate moments, the fixed glare can be a powerful weapon to keep order; but it should not be used to dominate, or to bend the meeting to the Chair's will. It is not a coincidence that Hitler was said by those who met him to have overpowered them with his stare. Violent criminals do the same to their victims.

If you are chairing the meeting, restrict your looking to brief eye contact with the members, one after another; this lets them know that you are equally interested in all of them and what they have to say.

Avoiding all eye contact suggests that either you have something to hide or you feel vulnerable and are desperate to defend yourself. Whether Chair or ordinary member, those are not the kind of messages you want to be sending out to your colleagues; so maintain eye contact throughout the meeting, but keep it easy and natural.

Behaving

How we want to be seen and treated by others depends on how we present ourselves – the way we talk, the way we dress, but especially the way we behave, i.e. our body language. From the moment we enter a room we are being judged. It is therefore up to us to make the most of the opportunity.

Whether we are running or attending a meeting, or standing about waiting for the meeting to commence, we do not want to be seen as timid, lacking in confidence, and unsure of why we are there or what we are doing. To be treated with respect we have to present ourselves as alert, confident, businesslike and purposeful.

Here is how to do it:

Dress appropriately

If the meeting is casual and you come in your best outfit, you will appear out of place, as though you are striving too hard to make an impression. If the meeting is formal and you come in casual clothes, you are either trying too hard to draw attention to yourself, which could be counter-productive, or asking to be treated as of no consequence. Spectacles, by the way, are supposed to give the appearance of possessing high intelligence.

Stand 'at ease'

Stand with legs slightly apart, hands by your side. Slouching signals nervousness and lack of confidence. Oddly enough, so, too, does an upright, rigid stance. Men should avoid keeping their hands in their pockets. Coin-jiggling is definitely out. For both men and women, holding a 'prop' like a briefcase can help make you look businesslike (as well as carrying all your important papers).

Sit comfortably

Sit close to, but not right up against, the table. Sitting at a distance signals lack of interest; too close suggests tension. Lean slightly back, because this gives an air of alertness and command; too far back may be a sign of boredom or lack of interest. Lean forward when you are about to speak. Do not cross your arms, which is a defensive gesture, and avoid encroaching on those sitting next to you because they will resent you invading their territory.

Keep your hands visible

Your hands should be on, or close to, the table. Keep them still except, of course, when you are writing. Fidgety fingers means nervousness, tapping fingers, annoyance. Try not to get into the doodling habit. We usually doodle when we are bored – which may not be the signal you wish to give to your Chair or to the other members.

Keep your hands away from your face

Hiding your face is a sure sign of lack of confidence. If you hide your eyes while someone is speaking to you, he or she cannot see how you are responding and will soon stop. If you hide your mouth when you speak, others cannot hear what you are saying; and if they can they possibly won't believe you, because you appear not to believe in yourself.

Listening

When you chair a meeting, listen more than talk. The less you say, the more the members can contribute, and in the end that is what will make the meeting a success.

Look at people while they are talking to you. You do not have to fix them with a stare as this will only make them anxious, but make frequent eye contact with them and they will respond to you more warmly.

The way you listen alters not only how a member addresses the meeting, but also what he or she says. Adopt an alert, slightly forward position, and the speaker (who will probably be glancing at you frequently) will respond to your interest by making an interesting contribution. Sit far back from the table and fix your eyes on some distant point in the room, and the speaker, unless full of self-confidence, will become hesitant, start to stammer, or go completely off the track. (If, of course, that is what you wish to happen, you now know how to do it.)

Your expression should indicate interest in what is being said, not who is speaking. If, therefore, your eye contact is too lingering, it may mean that you are interested in him or her on a personal rather than professional level. You may not, in fact, take in much information, because you are more concerned that the speaker rewards your admiring gaze with one of their own.

Listening is not enough; you must also *show* you are listening by your facial expressions and, more important, by nodding your head from time to time as this reinforces eye contact; so, too, does the slight tilt of the head which indicates thoughtfulness.

Because we listen at least four to five times faster than most people speak, we are always thinking ahead of the speaker though not necessarily about what is being said. We turn our thoughts to other matters that are on our minds or we daydream. We can, however, use these 'spaces' to review what the speaker has said, to evaluate the arguments, and to anticipate the conclusions so that we can prepare to counter them with our own arguments.

Good listening means listening to what the speaker is actually saying, not hearing what we would like them to say. When we listen we so often put up barriers of understanding between us and the speaker, barriers of bias and prejudice. Therefore, if we like the speaker, we tend to interpret everything they say in a favourable way, just as the crowd at a political rally will cheer to the rafters every cliché and banality uttered by their leader. Similarly, if we are prejudiced against the speaker, nothing he or she says will meet with our approval.

Good listening also means hearing what is *not* being said, in other words, the meanings the speaker may or may not be aware of. This is of particular importance if you are chairing the meeting, because if you miss the hidden messages you may also miss the plots hatching, the conflicts brewing, or the cliques and conspiracies forming; and it may be too late to do anything about them by the time you do discover them.

To be fully involved in a meeting, either as the Chair or an ordinary member, we have to train ourselves to listen without the barriers, to hear what is said, not what we would like to hear, and to respond accordingly, otherwise the flow of communication, so necessary to the success of the meeting, is obstructed and perhaps choked off for good.

Types and purposes of meetings

■ *Types*

Meetings, no matter what their purpose, fall roughly into three main categories: at one extreme is the small, informal meeting called 'on the spur of the moment', and at the other is the large, formal meeting for which proper notice has to be given. Falling in between the two extremes is the regular, periodic meeting which is planned and prepared in advance, though perhaps not more than a day, and which is controlled by the Chair, who follows certain rules which are not so much stated as understood and accepted by the members. Ideally, this type of meeting is conducted in an open, informal, democratic way with everyone having an equal opportunity to speak.

All three types of meeting have their advantages and disadvantages and from them we can learn what is best and what should be avoided when conducting or attending our own meetings.

Impromptu, or ad hoc meetings
You know the kind. It's late. You're just about to leave for home

when the telephone rings and your boss says, 'Something's come up. Would you join us in my office for a few minutes.' And if you start to object, he adds coolly, 'I'd really like to have you there.' In other words, miss it at your peril.

Some managers swear by them and think they are the only meetings worth having and, it must be admitted, they do have their advantages. They are ideal for dealing with emergencies because they can be called by anyone with the authority and can take place almost anywhere. The number of people attending is usually small – it need not be more than two – so they are easy to organise. There is a suitable urgency about them and the members are motivated to come to quick and appropriate decisions.

However, these meetings probably have more disadvantages than advantages. They are unplanned, and neither the person who calls the meeting nor those who attend will have done any preparation which means that, even though there is an emergency, time may be wasted.

Rule: the more valuable members are to the meeting, the less available they will be. Knowledgeable individuals who would make the most useful contributions to the meeting are not always there when you want them and, in their absence, unsafe decisions may be made.

As these meetings are probably held in an office or somewhere even more public, it is almost impossible to keep out interruptions like telephone calls and visitors. Constant distractions cause lack of concentration which may result in faulty decisions. Finally, the person who calls the impromptu meeting probably has not worked out an agenda. Without an agenda the meeting has no structure, and without a structure it can quickly become aimless or disorderly. Either way, it has been a waste of everyone's time. Yet, despite all this, most meetings fall into this category, which is why they are so unpopular.

Formal meetings

These are special meetings that you will only be invited to if you belong to organisations that are required to have them by law or by their own internal regulations. Unlike impromptu meetings these are planned in detail.

The rules under which they are organised will stipulate when they have to be held, what the agenda must contain and how soon before the meeting notice of the meeting must be sent out, usually together with the agenda. As a result, members are able to come prepared to make an informed contribution. The starting and finishing times are laid down in the agenda and strictly adhered to.

The timing for each item will also have been calculated by the Chair, which means that long-winded members are prevented from making interminable speeches. Rules of debate also prevent people from speaking repeatedly on the same subject. For all these reasons, formal meetings, when appropriate, can be very useful functions.

They too have disadvantages. Too much structure inhibits free and open discussion. Often these meetings are no more than a formality and members are required merely to give their assent to decisions made elsewhere. Occasionally, a small clique of dissenters will try to upset the smooth running of the show to give vent to their feelings or create publicity for their cause, though they are invariably overruled by the majority.

Formal meetings tend to go on for too long. Despite the imposition of strict time limits, their agendas often have to cover too many subjects. After a while members stop concentrating and will vote, not out of conviction, but just to keep things moving.

There are usually no surprises. Everything has been worked out down to the last detail, so little room is left for spontaneity, which can make them predictable and tedious. Anticipating this, the brightest and most useful members stay away, leaving the floor to the dull and boring, which only adds to the tedium.

Many members are invited because of their status or because the rules require their presence, so they come not out of interest but out of a sense of duty. The sheer size and importance of the audience will daunt all but the boldest from contributing to the proceedings.

Finally, decisions are taken by majority vote which means that there may be a sizeable minority who resent the fact that their views have been rejected.

Regular, periodic meetings
Staff meetings, review boards, committees of heads of departments, interdepartmental meetings, union – management committees, these and many more come under this heading.

Their regularity makes them ideal for any business that needs recurrent attention, and decisions made or solutions found at one meeting can be reviewed at subsequent meetings. The members know each other, they share a common history and they may even sometimes share common goals, which gives them a strong sense of identity.

If they are well run the members enjoy themselves, so absenteeism is low and productivity in terms of business covered and decisions made is high. If kept flexible, they should limit the number of impromptu meetings because they can identify and deal with trouble before it becomes an emergency. If they are fully integrated into the daily running of the organisation, they make it possible for management and workforce or senior and junior management to talk to each other in an unthreatening, unintimidating environment where views can be exchanged with relative frankness. They can therefore be valuable safety valves, preventing pressure from building up and exploding into serious industrial or management conflict. They are also ideally placed for reviewing new policy and procedures made elsewhere.

As they are informal, rules of procedure can be kept to a minimum. They are at a fixed time on a fixed day, so notices do not need to be sent; those who can come, do, those who can't are not penalised. Though there is an agenda, the Chair can be more flexible and introduce new items or cancel others if thought necessary. Minutes will be kept and circulated but these will be informal as will the proceedings, encouraging diffident members to make their contribution.

However useful, the main problem about the regular committee meeting is that, after a while, it begins to lack a sense of urgency. If it met last month and knows it will meet again next month, it will avoid making a decision this month. Carried on like this for too long and the committee ceases to have any purpose at all, which, unfortunately, does not mean that it will declare itself redundant, because by now the meetings will have become a habit for the members.

What started out as an effective group to tackle particular situations now becomes routine. The Chair and the members go through the ritual without putting much thought into it or taking much of use out of it. There is also the danger that the regular meeting may become too enjoyable. Every month members put off other, perhaps more urgent and important, tasks because they look forward to having a gossip with their colleagues even though, with each succeeding month, there is less and less real business to conduct.

Until someone, preferably the Chair, has the courage to face up to the fact that the committee has outlived its purpose, many cups of coffee will have been drunk, many plates of biscuits consumed and much time, effort and money wasted.

■ *Purposes*

From the definition of meetings we saw that they are the coming together of people for a purpose, and that defining the purpose is crucial to how the meeting is organised and run.

There are basically two main reasons for which meetings are held:

- Making decisions
- Solving problems

Other reasons for holding meetings are:

- Transferring information
- Negotiating
- Motivating
- Reviewing
- Making policy
- Delegating
- Presenting and selling
- Educating and training
- Creating ideas
- Establishing contacts
- Team building

Some general observations, or, is this meeting necessary?

1 Before you chair a meeting you should ask yourself: What do I want this meeting to achieve? By answering the question, you are establishing its purpose, and if you cannot answer it you ought not to call the meeting.

The reason for the meeting is not a secret only you know. It is something you have to pass on to the members, who should ask: What am I being required to achieve at this meeting? The answers to these two questions can be an area of potential conflict between the Chair and the members. If you have one idea of the meeting's purpose and the members have another, the meeting will fail.

2 Next you should ask yourself: Is this meeting necessary? To which you should add: Can the purpose be achieved more quickly and at less cost some other way? Since it is a fact that we take in far more data through the eyes than the ears, the transferring of information may be better achieved by sending it to the members than delivering it to them orally. Often meeting time is wasted clarifying new and complex data that have been introduced without warning instead of getting on with the main purpose, which is to make a decision on it.

3 Some meetings are called for more than one purpose. A training meeting may also involve motivating the trainees. A meeting to build a team may include some brainstorming. A sales meeting could also involve negotiating. The solving of a problem might establish new policy, and so on.

As long as the reasons are made clear and, moreover, are closely allied to one another there is usually no problem. It is only when the Chair wants to put into one meeting as many tasks as possible in order to save time and money that difficulties occur. If there are too many, the members may not know which one they are supposed to be dealing with and in the confusion may arrive at the wrong decision.

4 Can meetings generate fresh, original ideas, or are the two processes incompatible? The fashion for brainstorming meetings has been in decline since it was discovered that meetings are not necessarily the best medium for the creation of ideas. The individual sitting alone with thoughts, a pad or a computer, is probably far more effective than six or seven people throwing out unconsidered, unformulated notions.

Genuine brainstorming does not have an agenda or much of a structure, because it must be open and formless. To work properly there should be little or no distinction between leader and members, so the leader's role is not really that of a Chair in the accepted sense.

It is certainly possible to use meetings to *evaluate* ideas that have been conceived elsewhere, but, to be effective, such meetings should be conducted in the same orderly fashion as any other meeting.

5 Before embarking on yet another long session in a hot stuffy room, members should seriously ask themselves: Have I got enough information upon which to make a decision? Too often what appears a genuine meeting is only a rubberstamping ritual, because the members are not given sufficient data to embark on an informed discussion.

Typical of many companies is one with a large board of directors, consisting of the most senior and able men and women in the company, who meet every month supposedly to make policy decisions affecting the whole company. In fact all important decisions have already been made by the chief executive officers and the board merely agrees to everything put in front of them.

6 If you are about to chair a problem-solving meeting, ask yourself: Is the problem big enough to justify calling people away from their work, or can someone, the personnel officer for instance, solve the problem on her own?

If a meeting *is* necessary, then ask: Can I get the right people to solve the problem? Remember that they are usually those most in demand by other Chairs for other meetings. A third important question is: Is this the right time to call the meeting? Too often problem-solving meetings are called before the problem has become clear-cut enough to be solved, or they are called when the problem has already become a crisis. So good timing is essential.

At a problem-solving meeting the members should be directed to:

- Identify the problem
- Analyse it
- Consider various solutions
- Evaluate which one is best
- Come to a final decision, and
- Set a date for a further meeting to consider whether or not the solution has worked

7 Remember that the people you are dealing with are, like you, intelligent and independent, and that they much prefer to *agree* than to *obey*. This means that, to get them to come to your meeting, you

do not *command* them. You *negotiate* a convenient time and place. Unless, of course, you prefer to be surrounded by yes-men, there merely to cater to your whims rather than to give of their individual expertise and judgement. Which reminds me of a recent Piraro cartoon. The chairman, who is sitting in a huge chair, his left hand resting on a button on the table, is saying to the members seated around the large boardroom table, 'By now, those of you who voted "No" should be experiencing a steadily increasing sensation of warmth in the seat of your chair.' Small puffs of smoke are seen issuing from behind the chairs of some of the members.

8 Meetings are getting smaller and less formal, which is as it should be, because, as we've seen, formal meetings are only useful for certain very specific purposes whereas informal meetings are flexible enough to tackle almost any task. But the time is coming when meetings as we know them may no longer serve any useful purpose at all.

With the proliferation of the personal computer, office organisation is about to undergo enormous changes. People will spend more time with their computers than with each other. They may not even have an office, but conduct their business in the privacy of their homes and communicate with each other via computer. Whatever happens, it is probable that the rules for meetings will have to be completely rewritten.

8 What is the role of the Chair?

Before the meeting

You have decided to hold a meeting. You have also decided:

- What the purpose is
- Who is to come
- Where and when it is to be held

You (or your secretary) have carried out your formal duties of inviting the members and, if necessary, booking the room.

Now you have to decide what is to be discussed and in what order. In other words:

■ *The agenda*

Some Chairs claim they never bother with one. 'I just start straight in at any point and soon everyone joins in', is an attitude commonly found. But I suspect that, just as schoolchildren like to boast they have done no preparation for an examination when they have been swotting till all hours the night before, some managers think it makes them look superior to ordinary mortals who lack their natural gifts.

Why bother with an agenda? What can it do for you? Why can't you run a successful meeting without one? The answer is, you can, if the meeting has been called to discuss a single, straightforward item of business, for instance deciding which kind of fax machine to purchase. Once, however, you move away from simple decision making to anything even slightly more difficult, the need for an agenda becomes apparent.

What is an agenda?

An agenda consists of the items of business that have to be dealt with at a meeting; but, as we shall see, it is far more than that.

The agenda gives:

Direction

If you think of a meeting as a journey, then the agenda is the route map, and it follows that whoever is in charge of the map will know the directions and lead the others to their destination, namely, the purpose for which the meeting was called. This is your main duty as the Chair and if you fail to do this, the meeting has also failed. With an agenda, you stand a far better chance of succeeding.

Control

Rule: Uncontrolled meetings are unsuccessful meetings.
Problems of control often result from Chairs not knowing what they want from the members and members not knowing what is expected of them. With an agenda worked out in advance and circulated to the members, everyone is likely to enjoy the meeting more because they are involved in what is going on and are giving more to it, so control is no longer a problem.

Confidence

Think again of the meeting as a journey. If you start out without the slightest idea of where you are going, you are bound to feel apprehensive, and unless you can hide your own fears, your group will sense your apprehension and add to it their own. With a route map, you will be confident of where you are going and this will give the people you are leading confidence too, so that if you do have problems on the way, they can be confronted and overcome.

Purpose

Gathering half a dozen people in a room to talk aimlessly about different topics in no particular order is a highly inefficient way of running a meeting; and the chances of anything concrete or useful coming out of it are slim indeed. Yet this is frequently what meetings without agendas tend to be like. With an agenda the members know precisely what the meeting is about, and this alone will encourage them to work with you towards the same end.

The agenda is not a mere list of items, nor does it come out of thin air. You have to work at it, which may mean consulting others, reading relevant papers, or studying reports. It means thinking ahead, having the vision to anticipate problems, to see how the members will react to the various items that you intend to put down, what arguments they may advance against any of your proposals, what concessions you may have to offer them. Finally it means working out in advance how long the meeting is going to take so that you and the members can fit it into your schedules. Remember: *Meetings without an agenda can become meetings without an end.*

■ *How to plan your agenda*

For most formal meetings, the form of the agenda is usually set down either by the rules of the organisation or by how it has been done in the past, in which case you have little option but to follow precedent. In the formal agenda you always have to include:

- The title and/or purpose of the meeting
- Apologies from absent members
- Minutes of the last meeting
- Matters arising out of those minutes
- Any other business

With informal meetings, you, as Chair of the meeting, usually have a free hand to order the items for discussion in any way you wish. Uppermost in your mind should be to achieve the aims of the meeting in the most stimulating way, involving as many of the members as possible. So when you are planning the order of business, remember the rule: *The more is less and the less is more.* The more business you try to do in one meeting, the less you accomplish, so limit your tasks.

Ask yourself: How many and what items have to be dealt with? If you do not want the meeting to take up too much of your own and the members' time, you may have to limit either the number of items or the time spent on each.

What order should the items follow? This can be the trickiest question of all – the success or failure of the meeting depends on it.

Here are some points to consider: Ideally your aim is to motivate *all* the members to involve themselves in the discussion so that you end up with a consensus to which everyone has contributed. If none of the items is going to present any special problems, then, in order to maintain the interest of the members, you should vary them as much as possible.

Rule: A bored member is a potential time-bomb waiting to go off at the least provocation. Start with a couple of short items and follow them with a longer one; a less interesting item could come directly after one that has challenged the members, as this will give them the chance to recover before the next difficult one. However you choose to do it, the aim is to keep everyone interested.

The convenience of members is another consideration. The finance director whose input on whether or not to purchase another company is vital may have to leave the meeting early or arrive late, in which case you fit in that item on the agenda to suit his or her arrangements.

Start, if possible, on a positive note. There are few opening announcements better guaranteed to put members in an unresponsive mood than the Chair saying, 'I'm afraid I've got some bad news . . .', unless, of course, the news is the main purpose for the meeting. In this case it is better to say what has to be said so that the meeting can get on with dealing with the problem in a constructive manner.

Concerning items which are likely to cause dissension and division among the members, there are two schools of thought. One contends that they should be dealt with early on when the members are fresh and able to make useful, even if hostile, contributions to the discussion. The other holds that potential disagreements should be tackled later in the meeting when the members have less energy and enthusiasm to go at each other's throats. You have to make up your own mind according to the circumstances. My own view is that it is better to tackle problems when people are at their best, that is, earlier rather than later in the meeting.

The time of day the meeting is held can be important. Some Chairs prefer to call difficult meetings cither after lunch when the members are feeling replete and at one with the world, or late in the day when they are worn out from a day's work and want to gct home.

Depending on your own point of view, this is either clever strategy or low cunning which may succeed in disposing of the problem. In all likelihood, it will merely sweep the problem under the carpet.

Where possible, end your meeting as you began – on a positive note. Members, just as much as the Chair, like to feel that they have accomplished something and if the meeting ends positively they can go away thinking that their time was well spent. If, therefore, you have a potential dispute on the agenda, follow it with an item that will bring the members together again.

If the meeting is going to be long and complicated, you may find that you have to consult other members before you can finalise an agenda, in which case it is a good idea to circulate a draft agenda with a request for comments by a certain date. If you receive none, you can assume that the members agree with your draft.

A final point about preparing for the meeting: don't overdo it. Meetings are groups at work and if they are to function effectively and achieve what they set out to do, they should not only be organised and disciplined – which is what your preparation is designed to ensure – but also creative. In other words, there should be an element of risk, of chance, built into the meeting. As Chair it is part of your job to think ahead to what might happen; but if you work out in your mind a detailed scenario for every item in which you have all the answers to all the problems, you leave yourself no room to manoeuvre if matters take a course different from the one you anticipated. Not everything should be cut and dried, otherwise the meeting will be very boring for you as well as for the other participants.

Do you have a personal agenda? In other words, what, if anything, do you *personally* wish to achieve from the meeting? This may at first glance seem an odd question. Surely the reason to hold a meeting is for the good of the organisation you and the members serve? Well, yes and no. As human beings, we seldom do things only for others, no matter how unselfish and altruistic we may be. We are also motivated by self-interest. Some say we are primarily motivated by it.

As long as it does not go to extremes and turn to self-aggrandisement so that, instead of running meetings for the benefit of ourselves *and* our organisation, we run them solely to display or to increase our own power, there is nothing intrinsically wrong in self-interest. It can actually make better Chairs of us. Because we do not like to let ourselves down in front of others, we plan, organise and prepare ourselves for the meeting to make the very best impression. Everyone – ourselves, the members and our organisation – benefits from this.

At the meeting

The meeting is arranged, the members invited, and the room booked. What kind of meeting will it be? Will it be a success or a failure? Will it achieve its purpose? These are the kinds of question you think about before you chair a meeting and it is right that you do so, because, no matter how many meetings you have chaired in the past, every one is different.

The kind of meeting we run depends on the kind of people we are, because to a large extent our role as Chair is an expression and extension of our personality as a leader.

Basically, there are three types of Chair: the authoritarian, the permissive and the democratic. There are a number of psychological factors that distinguish them, but from the point of view of running a meeting, the distinctions can be summed up thus: The authoritarian does not want or like all the members to have a fair hearing; the permissive does not really care whether they do or not as long as he or she has a quiet life; the democratic positively wants and expects everyone to have a fair hearing.

Few of us fall exclusively into one category; most of us are a mixture of all three with more emphasis on one side of our character, depending on the circumstances. The normally permissive Chair, for example, who, for one reason or another, takes vehemently against one member becomes, as far as that member is concerned, a petty tyrant, ignoring him, arguing with him, or giving him little time to make his point.

None of us is perfect. We all have our faults and because they are an integral part of us we cannot leave them in the corridor outside when we enter the meeting room. Meetings are not unlike stage productions and we become, for the time we are there, actors acting out a role. In so doing, we can *choose* to act out our more positive and constructive characteristics and curb those that will impede the meeting. If, therefore, it is in our nature to be authoritarian, we can emphasise the more permissive side of ourselves and create a balance that will assist us in running our meetings more effectively.

All of us have some of the characteristics of the ideal Chair (see p.24). However, it does no good to worry too much about what you are lacking, especially as you are about to enter the meeting room, as this will only gnaw away at your self-confidence and limit your effectiveness as Chair. Much better to accept what you are and get on with the job of running the meeting to the best of your ability.

I said earlier that meetings resemble stage productions and as such they should have a beginning, a middle and an end. If we examine our functions and duties as a Chair at each stage we can see how our role changes and develops as the meeting proceeds.

■ *Starting the meeting*

The meeting starts for you sooner than for the members. If it is being held in a room other than your own office, however busy you are you should try to arrive a few minutes early to make sure:

- That there will be no distractions from noise, interruptions, inadequate lighting or heating
- That the furniture is comfortable (but not too comfortable) and arranged as you require
- That you have copies of the agenda and any documents sent to members before the meeting, because they often forget to bring them
- That everyone has writing pads and pens
- That, if visual aids are going to be used, they are in place and working, and
- That adequate refreshments are provided

Arriving early also helps you to prepare yourself psychologically for what lies ahead. It gives you time to calm unsteady nerves. If you have prepared yourself adequately, if you know your objectives and have worked out strategies to deal with potential problems, you should feel far more confident.

Everyone has their own methods of achieving inner calm, but I have found that if I think of myself as part of the group, not as the Chair upon whom so much depends, I relieve myself of some of the burden and place it on the meeting where, in reality, it belongs.

I also use deep breathing exercises to ease anxiety, and while I am doing them, I repeat to myself that the meeting is going to be successful and enjoyable. In this way I talk myself into believing it and usually I am right.

Whatever you use to ease tension, the one to be avoided is alcohol. As is well known, alcohol is not a stimulant but a depressant, and though it may seem to help in the short term, it reduces rather than increases efficiency. The control you think you are exerting over the meeting is illusory; in the long term its effects can be ruinous to health and career.

If the meeting is in your own office, you should still make sure that the room and the arrangements are in order. Don't forget to call your secretary or leave a 'Do not disturb' notice outside your door. Move away from your desk so that you are not seen as separating yourself from the others by the symbol of your authority. Arrange the chairs in an informal way. Make sure that all necessary documents are available, and if you haven't had time to circulate the agenda, have copies ready to hand out when the members come in.

Another good reason for being on hand before the start of the meeting is to greet the members as they arrive. The Chair who arrives late when everyone is already seated, unless he has a good reason, is most likely doing it to make an impression on the members, reminding them, in case they had forgotten, what a busy individual he is. The true impression they will gain, however, is that he is thoughtless and rude since their time is just as valuable as his.

In greeting members, there is no need to overdo the joviality. Instead of putting them at ease, it might make the more timid ones feel awkward and uncomfortable. Some writers recommend that Chairs know details of the members' personal lives so that they can 'break the ice', as it were, by asking the kind of questions that will show they are interested in them as people. I do not agree. Unless they know individuals reasonably well, personal questions will seem more like an intrusion into their privacy than genuine concern, and should therefore be avoided. Nevertheless, a pre-meeting chat about interests in common, accompanied by tea or coffee, can be a useful ice-breaker and help to get the meeting off to a good start.

Getting people to their places quickly in large meetings can be a problem, but is easily solvable by providing name plates. In smaller meetings the Chair or secretary can direct members to their seats, especially if you have worked out a particular seating strategy.

Now comes perhaps the most critical moment for you. In some ways you are like a schoolteacher entering a classroom for the first time. All eyes are on you and you are being judged. Do you know what you are doing? Are you or aren't you in charge? Will you be able to keep control?

It is now that you establish your authority. This is the moment, then, that sets the tone and mood for the rest of the meeting. The members will take their cue from you. If they sense that you are in charge, they will respond in like manner, and let you get on with the meeting, but if they feel by the way you present yourself that you are uncertain, unconfident, and perhaps a little frightened of them, they will, if they wish, take advantage of your fears and make life hard for you.

The key word is *Presence*. The positive image you present to the members by the way you walk, sit, talk, by the clothes you wear and the expression on your face is of someone who is friendly, confident, businesslike and purposeful.

Here are some hints how to achieve presence:

Prepare yourself well

If you have done your homework; if you know what the meeting is for and what you intend to accomplish; and if you have worked out your agenda, you have little to worry about, because you have already proved to the members that you know what you are doing. You can therefore begin in a calm, businesslike manner; brisk but not hurried, friendly but not hearty.

Start on time

This conveys the message that you have begun as you intend to carry on. Do not wait for late arrivals. If they are expected to make important contributions to items on the agenda, it is better to change the order of business – with approval of the other members – than penalise the punctual.

Introduce the members

Chairs sometimes take it for granted that, because they know all the members, everybody knows everybody else. In particular, introduce new members or visitors who may be too embarrassed to introduce themselves. This is also the moment to introduce your secretary, if he or she is present to take notes. Make sure you get the names of the members right. I was once rightly criticised by a member of a committee which I was chairing because I insisted on addressing him familiarly as 'Bob' when his proper name was 'Robert'. If you have any problem remembering names, make a plan of the table with the names of the members in the appropriate places. A glance at this will remind you who sits where.

Project your voice

Speak distinctly. Voices pitched low tend to carry more authority than high-pitched voices (listen, for instance, to the voice-overs in radio and television commercials), and a little training with a voice coach can help you to lower your tone if you have problems in that regard. You do not have to shout to be heard; speak at a good pace, neither too fast nor too slow, and articulate clearly. If members have to strain to hear what you are saying their attention will soon start to stray.

Get the business of the meeting started as quickly as possible.

The more time you give members to settle down, the longer they will take. At formal meetings Chairs sometimes use gavels to call the members to order, but in informal meetings this should not be necessary. If you appear alert and keen to get started, members will usually respond, but if not, give them 10 to 15 seconds before declaring the meeting open in a firm and, if necessary, loud voice.

Set the scene.

If you are nervous, the sooner you hear the sound of your own voice, the sooner you will start to relax. Concentrate on what you are saying, not on the impression you are making. In your opening remarks avoid the temptation to make speeches. Do not prejudge or express any opinions on issues still to be discussed. Stick to the facts and be brief. First, thank the members for attending. Courtesy costs nothing. Second, state the purpose of the meeting. The members may well know what it is, but repeating it gives immediate focus to the discussion. Third, whether or not they have seen the agenda, tell them what it is and obtain their agreement to it. If changes are proposed, accede to them if they will improve the running of the meeting since the agenda now belongs to the meeting. Fourth, state when the mecting will end.

Open firmly

Without further ado, introduce the first item on the agenda. Give the background – facts, please, not opinions – then open the discussion by inviting the members, one by one, to speak to it. You might remind them at this stage, if you have not done so earlier, that they should limit their contributions to, say, one minute, and you or your secretary should ensure that they do. Rather than open the discussion yourself, you may wish to call on the member who is closest to the subject to do so, in which case you should have arranged this beforehand so that it does not come as a surprise to the member.

Taking charge right from the start in this firm, businesslike manner sends out the clear message that you are in command of the meeting.

A brief note on taking notes

Before the business of the meeting starts, you should remind members that a record is being kept by you, your secretary, or by one of the members, who has volunteered to do so.

Taking notes at a meeting ensures that you and the members agree on what was decided there. Memories are faulty and unreliable, so it is much safer to have independent evidence of the proceedings. At formal meetings notes of both the discussion and the decision have to be fairly full, because the minutes circulated to the members afterwards are based on them. At informal meetings, though minutes are just as essential, they can take different forms, from a brief 'decisions only' note made by the Chair to an item-by-item record taken by the secretary with brief summaries of the suggestions and points made by the members in the discussion.

■ Running the meeting

The meeting has at last got under way and you are in charge. Its failure or success depends on a number of factors, the majority of which are in your control.

Moses had it easy. He had only one set of Ten Commandments to obey. Chairs have two sets: ten specific commandments as you work, item by item, through the agenda, and those ten general commandments that apply to all Chairs at all meetings.

Glancing at them, you may be forgiven for thinking that it is impossible for one person to obey all these commandments and still follow what is going on. However, on closer inspection you will see that, directly or indirectly, they all point to the one goal: ensuring that the meeting achieves its purpose.

Ten specific commandments

1 Control the meeting by sticking to the agenda, item by item. Change its order only when essential and then only with the consent of the members.
2 Introduce each item in turn. Give it shape by explaining its purpose and why it is on the agenda. State facts, not opinions. Be concise, do not make speeches.
3 Call upon members one by one to speak. If a number indicate their wish to speak at the same time, place them in order so that they know when their turn is.
4 Avoid always calling on the same speakers. Diffident members may need encouragement and will look to you to give it to them. Do not let them down.
5 Separate each subject under discussion. Do not let them become so entangled with each other that members are not sure which particular item is being discussed.
6 Remember always to thank members after they have made a contribution, whether or not you agree with what they have said.
7 Make sure that all members have an equal chance to express their views on each item before going on to the next.
8 Clarify issues if they become obscure. If argument has led to confusion, it is your task to unravel the strands so that the members know what they are being asked to decide.
9 At the end of each item summarise what has been said and what decisions, if any, have been reached. If members have been delegated tasks to carry out after the meeting, make sure they understand what these are.
10 Keep the discussion to the time limits. Do not show favouritism by letting those you agree with have more time than those you oppose.

Ten general commandments

1 Keep the meeting moving and on course in a firm but polite manner. You need not be heavy-handed and authoritarian about this: you are not teaching a class of children.
2 Express yourself clearly and unambiguously, avoid jargon, in-jokes and references that may be known to only some of the members.
3 Listen to all the arguments objectively, do not prejudge issues, and

do not use the meeting as a mere rubber stamp for decisions you have already made.

4 Do not give important and less important matters equal time. Avoid becoming bogged down in any one subject, particularly if it is of interest to only some of the meeting, and keep your own contribution to a minimum.

5 Defend the weak against the strong. Some members abuse their status or authority by bullying others into accepting their arguments. Keep them in check otherwise the meeting will not accurately reflect the true feelings of all the members.

6 Keep a look-out for potential trouble, for a build-up of tension or a clash of personalities and deal with it when it appears rather than ignore it in the hope that it will go away.

7 Praise others, not yourself. It may seem unfair but do not claim credit for doing things that as Chair you are expected to do, including running a good meeting. If compliments are given, accept them graciously.

8 Keep calm even when provoked, using humour to deflect anger but not to attack members. Avoid sarcasm or personal references, and do not abuse your power by making any member a butt of your jokes.

9 Vary the pace. Some more complicated items will need closer attention than others. When you think an item has gone on for too long, or judging by the expressions on the members' faces that they are becoming bored, bring it to an end and move on to the next.

10 Finish on time. Keep an eye on the clock and speed up if necessary to make sure you do.

■ *Ending the meeting*

End the meeting on a positive note, if possible, and do not forget to thank the members for attending. You want them to leave feeling positive towards you and any future meetings you will hold.

The task of the members is to come to a decision. What do you do if the members go on arguing and debating without doing so?

Reaching a Decision by Voting

In formal meetings decisions are mainly arrived at by voting 'for' or 'against' a motion put by one of the members and seconded by another. Sometimes decisions are reached without formal motions but on a question put to the members by the Chair.

As a rule, votes are not taken at informal meetings, because it means that there will be winners and losers. The losers may still be a considerable minority and will possibly resent the fact that their views have been rejected. As a meeting is a group activity, the cohesion of the group is thereby endangered.

If, having been given plenty of time to argue the matter, the members still cannot reach an agreement, it is your duty as Chair to end the debate by suggesting taking a vote. This sometimes has the effect of making members come to an agreement. But if not, this is how to go about it:

- State clearly and succinctly the proposition to be voted on
- Ask the members to raise their hands first 'for' then 'against' the proposition
- Count the votes or have the secretary count them
- Declare which side has won
- Keep a record of the vote and the numbers, to avoid future disputes

In extreme cases you or the members may call for a secret vote, in which event the members cast their vote by writing on pieces of paper, which are handed to you or the secretary for counting.

Reaching a Decision by Consensus

As we saw above, in informal meetings voting is potentially divisive and should be used only as a last resort. Your duty is to help the members reach consensus, or, in other words, a general agreement. Though not everyone may agree to the proposition, they will not be so wholeheartedly opposed to it to resent its acceptance and perhaps cause trouble after the meeting.

- Leave time at the end of the meeting to ensure that all the members have expressed their views. Those who have not spoken should be asked to do so, since they cannot expect you or the other members to read their minds
- Summarise the arguments for and against, emphasising the areas of agreement and analysing those of disagreement so that the members can understand clearly what, if anything, still remains to be debated
- Keep your own opinions to the end of your summary. Some Chairs prefer not to express any opinions at all

unless asked by the members but, as they are part of the meeting, I think it only fair they should be given the same chance as everyone else

- If no agreement is reached, suggest taking a vote. This often has the effect of concentrating the minds of the members on the problem and resolving it by agreement

- Once agreement has been reached, you or the secretary should record it and read it back to the members to make sure that it is correct. Keep a record of the agreement in case it is needed for future reference

It would be unrealistic not to mention that, if the members are all subordinate to the Chair, he or she may be able to insist on a decision. If you are in that position, you should still try to reach consensus because the members are people you work with – possibly on a daily basis – and if all your meetings end with you making the final decisions, they will start to harbour resentment against you which may leak into other areas of joint activity and eventually cause problems.

Modern organisations are, or should be, democratically run and the idea that managers can solve all problems and make all decisions is now seen as antiquated and inefficient. If you've worked to make a team, let the team make the decisions. By doing so, you will be helping them to use their capacities to the full and thereby to realise their own potential.

9 What is the role of the members?

How to make the most of meetings

As organisations have become more democratic so meetings have become less formal. The role of the Chair has diminished as that of the members has expanded. Writers now talk of 'member-centred' meetings. The focus is now on the members and the central concern of the meeting is how much the members take from it rather than what the Chair accomplishes.

My own view is that a meeting is an outward expression of a group in action, and that both the members and the Chair have interrelating roles to play. The flow is from the Chair to the members and back again from them to the Chair, and so on throughout the meeting. If, at any point, the flow ceases and the meeting becomes fixed either on the Chair or on the members, then something has gone wrong. The Chair may be making a speech or the members have got themselves embroiled in an argument. Then, as we shall see, depending on the circumstances, it is up to either the Chair or the members to break the impasse so that the flow can start up again.

Though it may be obvious to most people that meetings cannot exist without members, there are still some managers who run meetings expressly for their own benefit and ignore the needs of the members. They almost begrudge the fact that they have to pay any attention to them, and regard their presence either as a necessary evil or as a boost to their egos. Members should try to resist being treated in this way though, realistically, they may not have much of a choice because of their subordinate status.

Some people will do just about anything to avoid meetings. They'll suddenly discover long-lost relatives on their deathbeds or dreaded diseases of their own, because they feel that their presence is somehow not as vital as that of the others, or that they have no useful contribution to make. 'You don't really want me there. I'm useless at that sort of thing', is a remark often heard.

For you who hate meetings and do not know why anyone should invite you, here are some cogent reasons why your presence is desired.

It may be that:

- You have special knowledge of a subject upon which a decision has to be made
- You need information which you can only (or more conveniently) obtain at the meeting
- Your status obliges the Chair to invite you
- You will be carrying out decisions taken at the meeting
- The Chair needs your support
- The Chair wants to impress you
- The Chair hopes for a favour from you
- You have a balanced view and your wise counsel is valued

Unfortunately, just as there are Chairs who want and expect nothing from the members, so there are members who go to meetings expecting that everything will be done for them and that all they have to do is to be present and possibly to vote when called upon to do so.

This is not the case. Members have duties, too, and because of the close relationship between them and the Chair, they follow reciprocal patterns.

Before the meeting

Check your diary

As soon as the invitation is received, check to make sure that you are free. You may have another appointment, in which case you have to decide which is more important, but do not double-book your appointments in the hope that you can leave one or both of them early. This is poor organisation of your time and can lead to problems (see 'At the meeting').

Notify the Chair or the secretary whether you are coming or not

Do this as quickly as you can because they may have to book the room and make arrangments for the catering. Also, if you are in difficulties, early notification will allow the Chair either to postpone the meeting or to rearrange the agenda to suit you.

Check for directions

If the journey is complicated, give yourself plenty of time so that you arrive at the meeting punctually and in a calm state of mind.

Study the agenda and accompanying documents

Just as the Chair has to prepare for the meeting, so have you. All too often members leave the reading of the documents until just before the meeting starts (or even once it has started) which means that they cannot take full advantage of all the relevant information to make their points effectively.

Identify items in the agenda that you may wish to speak on

Prepare yourself thoroughly. Do whatever research you may need to back up your arguments, and prepare what you want to say. You will not need to write down everything otherwise your contribution will be laboured and sound like a speech, but you should note down all the relevant points you wish to make.

Make sure that you will not be interrupted

While you are attending the meeting you should be interrupted only if there is a real and unavoidable emergency.

At the meeting

Arrive on time

Some people love to make an entrance and always manage to arrive once the meeting has begun with excuses about how busy they are. As a way of drawing attention to themselves it may work once or twice, but soon the other members will tire of it and treat the exhibition as a joke or a nuisance.

Wait to be seated

On entering the room, wait to be seated by the Chair or the secretary unless you know everyone well and are familiar with the seating arrangements. If you are a new member, coming into someone else's room and taking up a seat without permission makes you look arrogant or bad-mannered. Not a good way to start.

Organise yourself

You should be ready from the beginning to make a positive contribution to the meeting. Arrange your papers with the agenda on top so that you can easily put your hand on information or notes that you may want to use when speaking to any of the items.

Concentrate

Concentrate on the proceedings and be seen to be concentrating. The Chair will be glancing at you from time to time and so might the other members to see how you are reacting to what is going on. Do not slouch, gaze abstractedly up at the ceiling, or doodle on the pad, because these are clear signals that you are bored. If you want to make a positive impression, show enthusiasm and interest.

Address the Chair and the members formally

Use 'Mr', 'Mrs', 'Ms' – unless you are on first-name terms with them or have been asked to address them more familiarly.

Speak early

Speak first or as early as possible if you want to influence the course of the debate; but if you want to clinch the argument in your favour, speak last.

Help the progress of the meeting

Ask the Chair for a summary of what has been said when it goes off the track, or when it has slowed down; remind the meeting of the time; or ask for a decision when the discussion on an item has gone on for too long. These interventions should always be made in a polite manner without hostility or sarcasm.

Make a good impression

Conduct yourself in a friendly, positive manner. Members who are always complaining, who only have negative points to make, and whose attitude is one of superiority threaten the well-being of the group and for this reason are not welcomed.

■ *Stay until the end of the meeting*

Leave only if there is an emergency and you have no alternative, or if you have told the Chair in advance and have his or her consent. Just as some people like to arrive late, so some leave early for the same reason – to call attention to themselves. In both cases their actions are ill-mannered and selfish, because they disrupt the meeting and hinder its progress. If the meeting is running over time and the Chair ignores reminders, then the threat to leave may have the desired effect.

■ *Presenting yourself*

The three main reasons why people go to meetings are to participate in an activity of the group to which they belong; more specifically, to help the meeting achieve its purpose, and to get something out of it for themselves.

This last reason is thought to be too selfish a view, but it is, in fact, a healthy approach. Taking as much as you can from the meeting to further your career, or for whatever other apparently selfish reason, will encourage you to give far more of yourself as a member. By serving yourself, you are serving others.

Your best chance to shine at a meeting is by speaking, not by staying silent. Silence has its place, and there are times, as, for instance, when members are engaged in a fierce battle of wills, that remaining aloof can earn you far more Brownie points than throwing yourself into the fray. But this is an exception. It is only by speaking that you can command the attention and respect of the Chair and the other members.

Here are some hints to make sure that you do not waste the meeting's time or your opportunities. You may not have that many of them.

Speak only when you have something relevant to say

Gaining attention is fine, but you do not have to speak to every item and become the kind of nuisance who makes members groan inwardly every time you raise your hand. Members who always have something to say on every subject take up valuable time and ultimately hinder the work of the meeting.

Work out what you want to say preferably before the meeting has started

You can then obtain all the necessary facts to strengthen your argument. If, on the spur of the moment, you decide you want to contribute to the discussion, jot down a few points before indicating your intention to speak. This will give you time to gather your thoughts.

Speak quickly

Rule: slow talkers are boring to listen to, no matter how interesting their information. We take in information much faster than we speak – four to five times faster, in fact. If you present your material slowly, your audience will grasp the gist of your message and still have time to think of other things. You are also giving them the chance to assemble their arguments against you even while you are talking.

Raise your voice

Rule: A strong, clear voice carries information with conviction. Even in a quiet room, it is difficult and distracting for your audience to have to strain to catch what you are saying. If, in addition, you are competing with extraneous noise of telephones, traffic, the hum of lighting or air-conditioning, you will not be heard and your contribution will be wasted. Remember to keep your hands away from your face, because this stifles your voice and gives the impression that you are either uncertain or devious.

Make your key points as quickly as possible

Avoid long preambles. A sentence or two should be enough to raise expectations that something interesting is going to come.

Use words accurately

Avoid generalisations such as, 'always', 'never', 'everyone', as in, '*Everyone* knows that we *never* make concessions when negotiating and that's why we *always* win.' That may sound convincing to you, but not to listeners who may not share your views.

Support your views with facts

Opinions, no matter how forcefully expressed, carry only a certain amount of weight. Back them with evidence and you have a far better chance of winning the argument.

Take one point at a time

If you try to present all your arguments at one go, you will not only exhaust your supply but will also leave everyone totally bewildered. The procedure that good speakers adopt so that their audience can follow them is: (1) say what you are going to say; (2) say it; (3) then sum up what you have said.

Be calm

Shaking hands, a tremor in your voice, send out clear signals to your listeners that you are nervous, and sometimes people take advantage of the fact. Do not give them the chance. Prepare yourself well and take a few deep breaths before you start to speak. If your hands are trembling, do not pick up any papers. If your view is challenged by a member, do not take it personally but concentrate on the issues. That way you will avoid becoming angry and flustered.

Be bold

Faint heart never won fair lady, goes the old saying. Faint speakers never won any arguments, either. Believe in what you are saying and in your right to say it, and you will get others to believe in it too. If your voice tends to be on the high side especially when you are excited, try to lower it because, like it or not, deep voices carry more conviction.

Put your case positively

It is worth repeating that members whose contributions are always negative earn the reputation of being bad at meetings and by extension poor team members. Obviously there are bound to be times when you have to point out what is wrong rather than what is right with an idea or proposal otherwise you will be seen as a 'yes-man', which is also to be avoided. But if you criticise another's suggestion offer a positive alternative, not just, 'I'm against the idea of moving our offices', but, 'I believe we can get more out of what we've got here.'

Be balanced

In the end it comes down to taking the balanced view. Good common sense is not so common as one might suppose, and if you can be relied on to supply it you will always be welcomed at meetings.

10 What can go wrong with meetings (and how to put it right)

'To boldly go where no man has gone before', is the proud claim of Captain Kirk, the commander of the *Starship Enterprise* of television's *Star Trek* fame, and to some extent this is how every meeting sets off. Like Captain Kirk, the Chair and members know, or ought to know, more or less where they are going and have prepared themselves well for the voyage. What they do not know are the dangers they may face.

Meetings, like voyages through space, are strewn with potential problems. The Chair and the members, their sights set on a successful conclusion, have to guide their way through uncharted territory with care without at the same time becoming too obsessed with the difficulties, as to do so will only slow down their progress and even perhaps distract them to such an extent that what they fear worst will happen – the meeting will self-destruct somewhere in space. *Boldly* is the key word.

What follows is a handy guide to the most common dangers you may find yourselves facing on your journey either as Chairs or members, together with advice on what safety measures to take if you do.

Knowing something about how groups work is perhaps the best general precaution to take. One of the first tasks of a group is to survive and this survival instinct is something that both the Chair and the members can use to their advantage, because it will assist them not only to keep the meeting going when it seems most threatened by dissent, but also to return to a consensus.

One of the main ways the group survives is by exerting pressure on deviant or difficult individuals within it. This pressure should not be employed to crush all dissent, because the difficult or dissenting member, by challenging the group to think, can strengthen it and give it the kind of creative life it needs to fulfil its purpose. Usually the group is strong and cohesive enough to cope with dissent, but if the difficult member has more power than the others or more support within the group, he or she can wreak havoc on it.

This applies particularly to the Chair. If he proves to be the most difficult member of all, then the meeting is in trouble. But, as we shall see, members are not helpless. They, too, have power, and they can use it to exert pressure on the Chair and bring him or her to order so that the meeting can continue and achieve its purpose.

Here are ten most common problems that meetings have to face, and the steps that should be taken to deal with them.

- A bad start
- The dictatorial Chair
- Poor time-keeping
- Disruptions
- Loss of direction
- Domineering members
- Conflict and aggression
- Hidden agendas
- Having too much fun
- A poor finish

A bad start

According to surveys on meetings, ineffectual leadership is the problem most commonly experienced by members. This is often because the Chair has never really thought about how to conduct a meeting, believing, as so many do, that anyone with a modicum of intelligence can do it and that they, in particular, have a unique talent for the job.

Unfortunately, this is not the case. Chairing a meeting is, as I think I have amply demonstrated, fraught with difficulties. The skills required do not come naturally to most of us, but have to be learnt through training and experience. By reading this or, indeed, any book on meetings, those who find themselves having to chair a meeting will at least have taken positive steps to correct any glaring defects, and to improve skills which they have already acquired.

The errors that most clearly expose an ineffectual Chair are a messy start, and, as we shall see later, an inconclusive finish.

As the leader of the group, it is up to the Chair to set the tone and mood of the meeting from the moment the members gather in the room, and this should be brisk and purposeful. If, therefore, instead of getting on with the business, you waste time determining what the meeting is about, whether the right people or the right documents are available, and what decisions have to be made, you will find yourself faced by a group of justifiably irate people. You may have taken them away from more important business, and even if you haven't, they will have to spend an hour or more of time-consuming and boring discussion which will probably lead nowhere.

If, on the other hand, you have prepared well, you will have no difficulty presenting yourself effectively as someone who knows what to do. The members will respond in like manner and the meeting can get off to a businesslike start.

A question often asked by those new to the job of Chair is: will I make a good Chair if I know all the rules of debate? The answer is: no. Swallowing *Citrine's ABC of Chairmanship* whole may help if you have to chair a formal meeting but for informal meetings a detailed knowledge of procedural rules can actually slow things down.

The Chair who looks up the rules whenever there is a problem, who will not allow members to address each other but insists they 'speak through me', who requires proposals to be put in the form of a motion, or who wants a vote on every decision may get through the work of the meeting *eventually*, but at the risk of making himself very unpopular with the members.

Chairing a meeting is not a popularity contest, but to ensure that the meetings you run are not only effective but also enjoyable, so that people will come to them of their own free will and not out of duty or under compulsion, rules should be acceptable to all the members and be invoked only when absolutely necessary.

The dictatorial Chair

A difficult problem for many senior managers is separating their position outside the meeting room from that inside. They are tempted to use their ultimate weapon – the members' jobs – to force through decisions. But meeting to agree to a decision that has already been taken is a waste of company time; a memo would do the job more efficiently and would not, moreover, leave members with the uneasy feeling that they had been manipulated.

Fortunately, most managers resist the temptation to bully their subordinates because they realise that it is counter-productive. But there are other less obvious ways to force meetings to go where they want them to go. One is to keep the meeting moving at such a fast pace that no time is given for free discussion. The excuse is usually, 'We're all busy people so we don't want to waste our valuable time debating. Let's just come to a decision.' Because most people do not like to spend too much time at meetings, they readily agree and the decision goes through 'on the nod'.

Members should resist the Chair's attempt to drive through decisions in this way, especially when important issues are at stake that will affect their lives. It needs only one member to point out that they are moving too quickly to halt the headlong rush, because as soon as attention is drawn to it, the others will agree and the Chair will have to slow down.

Dominating Chairs ask members leading questions, such as, 'You do agree, don't you?', and, 'You've expressed similar opinions, not so?' Or suggestions like, 'I'm happy to go on talking about this for hours, but why don't we just try it my way and then see.' Put often enough, these suggestions and so-called questions can undermine the most determined meeting.

They also try blackmail: 'If we don't agree, I'll have to tell the board and it'll be up to them to decide.' Or what I call 'the misunderstood child' ploy: 'I don't understand why you're so against my idea.'

Once again, it is up to one member to point out to the Chair that the blackmail, the suggestions and questions are making it impossible to tackle the issues independently, and the other members only have to agree to exert sufficient group pressure for the Chair to mend his or her ways. Remember – there are always more of you than the Chair.

Some managers treat their meetings as opportunities for making long speeches which the members, especially if they are subordinates, have to endure. The Fidel Castro syndrome has to be resisted, but it takes courage, not of one but of all. It is unfair to expect one person alone to take on the responsibility of telling the Chair that he or she is wasting the meeting's time. Group pressure must be brought to bear on the speech-maker through body language, or, if the Chair is too obtuse to notice the boredom on faces, the shuffling in seats, the irritable tapping of fingers on the table, then in simple words of one syllable, for example, 'We'd like to sit here listening to you, but we will fall behind in our work if we do.'

Poor time-keeping

Chairs are primarily responsible for keeping good time, yet often they are the worst offenders. They arrive late; they start late; they take too long getting into the meeting; they allow discussions to ramble on; they do not get through the agenda; and they finish late. They also waste time by not giving the members the paperwork to digest before the meeting.

Rule: Keeping time is a group responsibility and a group achievement. Members can help to move the meeting forward by arriving punctually, by reading all the documents they have been sent, by speaking briefly and to the point. If discussions have gone on too long, they can ask either that the issue be put to a vote or that the meeting moves on to the next piece of business, and if the other members agree, the Chair will have to comply.

If the meeting is running over time, the members do not have to suffer in silence. They can request that it be brought to an end, and if the Chair takes no notice they can threaten to leave or, if necessary, walk out.

Disruptions

As we have seen, it is the Chair's responsibility to make sure the room is free from distractions and that the meeting will not be disrupted. However, in spite of all the precautions, disruptions sometimes do occur. Perhaps the most frequent is the late arrival of a member. If, as Chair, you have been forewarned and you pass this on to the members at the start of the meeting, then, when this member arrives, disruption is kept to a minimum. If you have not received any warning, then the less notice you take of the late arrival the better, especially if it is an entrance staged for effect. Do not listen to excuses or explanations until the end of the meeting.

If you are dealing with a persistent late-comer, you can make it a group issue. Get all the members to understand and agree that punctuality is essential to the success of the meeting.

Similarly, if a member is called away in the course of the meeting, ignore it. Drawing attention to disruptions when they occur only exacerbates them. Embarrassing a persistent wrongdoer in front of the other members by pointing out their wrongdoing can be a very effective way of calling them to order, but only at the end of the meeting, perhaps under 'Any other business'.

Loss of direction

It is in the nature of groups to take the line of least resistance, to go for easy options and to avoid making hard decisions. If not reminded from time to time of their goal, they will lose sight of it and forget why they have met and what is expected of them. As a result, they become bogged down in irrelevant, time-consuming discussions which lead nowhere.

What can you do to bring the meeting back on track?

■ *Refocusing*

As Chair, when you realise that the meeting is losing its way, stop and remind the members of the reason why you met. 'We're here to decide whether or not to install a new computer system, not to discuss the quality of the computer operators, which we seem to have strayed into.' By doing so, you will be refocusing the meeting on its task.

■ *Summarising*

As an ordinary member, if you sense that the meeting has lost its way, you are at liberty to intervene in the discussion with a summary of the points that have already been made. 'Have I got this straight? Our operators are finding that our present system isn't flexible enough because . . .'. So long as your intervention is made in a straightforward, businesslike manner, without impatience or implied criticism, the Chair will welcome it.

■ *Limiting the number of tasks*

Remember, as Chair, by limiting the number of tasks you ask your meeting to accomplish, you have a better chance of maintaining your focus right through the meeting. The more you try to tackle, the more likely you are to get in a muddle. Set a brisk pace right at the start, but if you see that you will not get through the agenda, either speed up or postpone the less important items until another meeting – with the consent, of course, of the members.

Domineering members

Just as the Chair can dominate a meeting and push through decisions so can individual members, especially if they are in a more powerful position than the others, or if they are held in awe because of their knowledge or expertise in the subject under discussion. The problem is made more acute if you, as Chair, share the meeting's feelings towards the member in question and are therefore inhibited from exerting control.

Your duty as Chair is to give everyone a fair chance, but how can you do so in these circumstances without offending the domineering member?

The answer, as so often is the case, is not to fight the battle alone, but to use group pressure. Thank the member in question for his contribution then bring in the others. 'We've all heard what Gordon has said, now I'd like to ask the rest of you for your comments.' You have to do this quickly and firmly otherwise you risk having him pushing in and demanding a decision without further discussion. If you do this each time he speaks, he will soon get the message that you are not going to let him get his way and take over your meeting.

I am not saying this is easy, but it is essential if you want to save yourself and your members from being forced along a route that you would not freely choose.

Conflict and aggression

The central problem of running a meeting is that you are required to strike a balance between allowing everyone to express their views freely and, at the same time, maintaining control, and to do both while keeping your sanity and their respect. The job is made doubly difficult if the members are hostile to you, to each other, or to the proposals under discussion.

It is not surprising that some managers shy away from so daunting a task and others take it on in the hope that either the problem will go away or that somehow they can keep the lid on the strong emotions that might be expressed.

Problems, however, do not go away and feelings suppressed at meetings inevitably come out elsewhere, possibly where they can do more harm. If members, encouraged by the Chair, are more concerned to be polite to each other than to express themselves freely then the real, substantive purpose of the meeting is unlikely to be achieved. The Chair may end up with some kind of agreement, but not one that accurately reflects the true feelings and opinions of the members.

Meetings are ideal places for releasing hostility and you have to be tolerant of anger and disagreement. In preparing for the meeting, try to envisage which issues are most likely to cause dissension and allow these items more time. Then, as long as the combatants do not go off the subject, or beyond the allotted time, or engage in personal abuse, let them speak their minds.

You do not have to intervene except as mediator or, as one executive put it, 'Stop the warring parties shouting at each other from the mountain tops and bring them down to the valley floor again to talk.'

One of the best ways to do this is by summarising. ('If I have understood you correctly, Antony, you say the orders haven't been coming through fast enough, and you, Mike, think they have.')

Summarising allows a pause in the proceedings which gives the combatants a chance to calm down; it also puts the meeting back on track if the arguments have thrown it off. By appealing to the other members you can use the pressure of the group to restore order. ('I think Antony and Mike have got themselves into a no-win situation. Would anyone like to suggest how they can get out of it?')

If emotions have become too heated, you might consider taking a short break for coffee, and if that does not work, you might have to adjourn the meeting, or at least postpone the items that are causing the problems.

Whatever steps you take, do not:
– abdicate control so that the meeting drags on. This is unfair on, and extremely uncomfortable for, those not involved in the conflict. They have to wait on the sidelines while the combatants fight it out to the bitter end, or
– take sides in the argument. That way you lose all objectivity and consequently your role as mediator is compromised, perhaps fatally.

What do you do if one of the members becomes aggressive and unruly? What you do *not* do is argue with him; that will get you nowhere. Instead, try the silent treatment. Silence can be more eloquent than words. Wait until he has finished his tirade, then, rather than jumping straight in with a response, sit quietly for a few seconds and let your silence show your own and the meeting's disapproval of his behaviour. A steady gaze on the offender can add weight to the message.

Should that not work, you can call him to order. 'There is no need to shout, we can all hear you perfectly well, and I'd also ask you to sit down.'

If he still persists in trying to upset the meeting, you can divert attention from him by appealing to the other members. 'I think we all understand Ralph's point, but we have other matters to attend to and I'd like to move on, if everyone agrees?' It is unusual in these circumstances for members to disagree, because they, too, have had to suffer from the unruly behaviour and are just as eager as you are to put a stop to it.

If one member still persists in disrupting the meeting, you have no choice but to ask him to leave, and if he refuses, bring the meeting to an immediate end. You can adjourn or postpone it to a time when the member is either absent or has calmed down.

Hidden agendas

The hidden agenda or secret objective is different from, and invariably opposed to, the one proposed and accepted by the rest of the meeting. The Chair or a member can follow it.

Not all hidden agendas are harmful. Some, in fact, can be quite beneficial as when, say, ambitious Chairs seeking promotion conduct themselves in their meetings so efficiently that someone higher in the organisation notices them. Everyone benefits from that and it is only when they start to hold more meetings than are strictly necessary in order to draw attention to themselves that their secret ambition becomes counter-productive.

Other hidden agendas are either too trivial ('why do we always meet in *her* room, why not in mine?') or too remote from the purpose of the meeting ('I don't really care whether or not we change our timber suppliers; I want to change the wallpaper in this office.') to warrant much attention.

Hidden agendas come in many forms: one member wants the job of the Chair, another is trying to discredit a rival, or is riding a favourite hobby-horse; another is getting rid of frustrations that have been building up. Whatever the cause, if ignored they can be a virus that will eat into and destroy the healthy body of a meeting. A grudge, say, between two members can subvert any discussion, no matter what the subject, until the meeting grinds to a halt. As long as the grudge persists the members will go from meeting to meeting, turning debates into personal battles.

How do you spot a hidden agenda? This is not always easy, because not even the individual may consciously be aware of its existence. It takes insight and empathy, as well as the ability to read people's body language. For example, the member who, by the way she sits or stares into space, seems not to be part of the meeting until a particular item is mentioned then is suddenly alert and animated may be using that item to express some hidden ambition. Persistent lateness may be a signal to the Chair that the member is unhappy with the way he or she is being treated at the meeting.

Personal agendas also hide behind the words people use, and listening to what the speaker is saying, as well as to what he is *not* saying, can reveal them. 'I wonder why my ideas are so seldom accepted?' can mean, 'I am not being appreciated.' 'I notice that accounts are getting a new carpet, again' is saying, 'Accounts are treated better than my department.'

Chairs who know which members are bringing their own secret objectives into the meeting can prepare themselves to deal with the problem, should it arise, highlighting again the importance of good preparation.

Some agendas are hidden so deeply that without the gift of second sight you will not be able to anticipate them and they will only start to reveal themselves in the course of the meeting. You then have the choice: ignore it and hope it will go away, or expose and confront it.

Depending on how important the objective is to the member, the first approach sometimes works. If it is not important, you can suggest moving on to the next topic in the hope that the member concerned may forget it or put it aside for another occasion. But this approach is seldom the best. Members will often persist until they achieve their objective, and in doing so they may ruin your meeting. Far better to bring the hidden agenda into the open for all to see, and let the meeting decide what to do about it.

If you think that Anita is out to build an empire for herself and is not accepting any decisions that threaten her plans, you might say, blaming yourself, 'I'm sorry, Anita, but I don't understand why you're objecting to the company taking on extra staff.' She is unlikely to admit her real reasons for objecting, but is forced to come out with some explanation. 'I don't object to more staff, but I think they should be in my department.' Your response now is to draw in the other members by asking them what they think. 'I'd like to ask the others what they feel about this. Do you think Anita's department should get the new staff?' Their discussion will inevitably expose her real objectives and by exposing them, put an end to them.

If two or more members share an agenda, you have a conspiracy on your hands, which can be even more difficult to tackle. To attempt to do so on your own is foolhardy, because they have the advantage of numbers, and will take the meeting over if you let them.

The members not in the conspiracy are your potential allies, so address yourself to them. 'We don't seem to be making any progress. Does anyone know why?' Ask each member for an answer until the conspiracy is exposed as it will be by the time you have gone round the table. You can then ask how they think the problem can be dealt with.

Having too much fun

Meetings are work, or they should be, otherwise they are a waste of time. But that does not mean that they should not be enjoyable. On the contrary, the more members enjoy the meeting, the more they will put into it: enjoyment, however, in the sense that they are completely absorbed and involved in what is going on, and feel satisfied that they are doing a useful job.

Where the Chair and the members all know each other well, there is a danger that being together becomes an end in itself. The Chair ceases to take the lead, discussion degenerates into conversation, whatever the ostensible purpose was for calling the meeting is forgotten, and nothing is accomplished.

The Chair is primarily responsible for permitting this to happen, but all should be on guard against it. A tight agenda, a fixed time limit, a definite purpose, and the minimum of refreshments should ensure that the meeting remains what it set out to be. The introduction of alcohol is a danger signal and should always be avoided.

A poor finish

Indecisive endings leave everyone low-spirited and disappointed and the blame for this is usually laid firmly on the way the Chair conducted the meeting.

The causes for meetings ending badly are numerous, but the two most common are:

- Not defining its purpose
- Trying to tackle too many subjects

The solutions to both are simple:

- Know precisely why you are calling the meeting, and if there is a more efficient way to reach the same result, use it
- Do not attempt to solve all the world's, or your organisation's, problems at one go. Take one issue at a time

Whatever problems you encountered as the Chair in the course of the meeting, members should be left feeling that their time was well spent and that it would be a pleasure not a penance to attend your meetings in the future.

They will do this only if you moved at a good pace, if the debates were lively yet serious, if you dealt with any problems in a calm, businesslike manner, if the agenda was covered within the time agreed and, most important, if the meeting ended conclusively and on a positive note.

11 What happens after the meeting?

The story continues . . .

- A meeting is part of a process. What happens at the meeting depends on what has gone before. What happens afterwards depends on what happens at the meeting itself. This leads to new developments which, in turn, lead to more meetings, and so on.

- A meeting should not be an end in itself. If it is, it means that either the reason for calling it is trivial, or someone, the Chair most probably, is using it to serve his or her own ends.

- A meeting is always for a purpose which is defined before the meeting and is carried out after the meeting has finished.

- Actions decided upon at a meeting, if left for too long, tend to lose their impetus and remain undone. Repeated failure to act upon decisions eventually affects the morale of the members to the detriment of the group as a whole.

- Prompt action taken after the meeting when members are still enthusiastic assures greater success which encourages their involvement in future meetings.

- Actions taken on decisions can only be carried out if they are based on a realistic knowledge of the circumstances in which they have been made. For example, a decision to move offices involves answering a number of questions: does the meeting have the authority to make such a decision? If so, has the organisation the money to meet the cost of removal as well as making voluntary redundancy payments to those who choose not to go? Thirdly, what do the staff think about the move; have they been consulted? Failure to take these questions into consideration when making the decision will result in unnecessary confusion and, more important, a very unhappy workforce.

- Before arranging a meeting, the Chair should make sure:

  - That the limits of its authority are clearly defined
  - That it has the resources to carry out its decisions
  - That those affected by the decisions have been consulted

- A final point for the Chair to consider is how a decision taken at the meeting will affect the organisation as a whole. As a stone thrown into a pond causes ripples that touch all sides of the pond so a meeting may affect all sections of an organisation. This being the case, the Chair should ensure before all important meetings that those who have the overall responsibility of the organisation know what it is about, who is to attend, why it is being held, and what decisions the Chair hopes will be taken.

Keeping a record

Decisions made at meetings should always be clear and unambiguous otherwise members will not know precisely what is expected of them. Unfortunately people's memories are notoriously unreliable, which often leads either to tasks being forgotten or disputes arising over who is to do what. If you want to be sure that decisions made at your meetings are carried out by those appointed to do so, record them in writing.

In formal meetings, as we have seen, these records are called minutes and they follow a certain form. For informal meetings all that is required is a note of the decisions which have been agreed upon, what action is required and who is to carry it out. If thought necessary, the record could also contain the more important arguments raised in the discussion as well as suggestions made about future action.

Some organisations like to keep a meetings book recording the nature of the meeting, the date when it was held, who attended and what decisions were reached. I know of one organisation that likes to video-record all its meetings. The advantage of this is that there will be no doubt about what happened and what decisions were made; but I think the presence of the recorder inhibits free discussion, because people will be thinking, not of what they are saying, but who will see the tape when the meeting is over.

The way decisions are recorded is less important than their accuracy and the promptness with which they are circulated to the members. The longer it takes for a note to be sent around, the greater the chance that the members will have lost interest in doing what was required of them. A couple of days after the meeting should be ample.

The responsibility for checking the accuracy of minutes or notes and sending them out rests with the Chair. If he or she has a secretary, it is important that they sort out between them who is to do what otherwise each may leave it to the other, and it will not get done.

The Chair's work is never done

So it will seem, if you are the Chair of a committee that meets regularly. When everyone else has packed up and gone, you have more duties to perform, as vital as those before and during the meeting. And just as you controlled the meeting, so you have to control its outcome to ensure that the tasks are carried out.

It is important that you do not take on too many duties. Groups are always happy to flog a willing horse, and if you volunteer to do all the work arising from the decisions, the meeting will not stand in your way.

Delegating not only relieves you of some of the burden, it is also the best way to test your team's abilities and to show that you trust them.

There are, however, some duties you should not delegate, or if you do, only to your secretary whose experience in these matters you trust. These concern firstly, the minutes or the record of decisions. Alone, or together with your secretary, you will draft, check and make certain that they have been circulated as soon as possible, preferably within two or three days after the meeting. You will then check to make sure that those tasks that have been delegated are being carried out.

Unless the tasks are of great urgency, you or your secretary should err on the side of caution, because if they have been voluntarily undertaken you will not get the members' co-operation by nagging them. If they also happen to be busy people in positions of power, you will be doing yourself a disservice, bringing the meeting's functions down to a personal level. There will be another meeting when they will have to face the disapproval of the group if they did not carry out what they promised.

As a member you should also not volunteer for all the jobs going, because no one will stop you. You will then find yourself overwhelmed with work, and, instead of enjoying what you have undertaken and performing it with relish, you will come to resent it, probably do it badly, and as a result earn not applause but jeers.

I am not saying you should never volunteer. Apart from the experience and goodwill you gain, it is a good way of being noticed. *The rule is: do not over-extend yourself.*

The end of the story?

Meetings are essentially office-based. Senior management may spend up to fifteen hours a week attending them; middle and junior management only slightly less. The cost is enormous. The reason there are so many meetings is that they are so easy to arrange. People are easy to get hold of and, more important, are within walking or easy travelling distance of the meeting room.

That, however, is changing. The bottom line for businesses is costs, and running an office with its continually rising overheads is an expensive undertaking. Information technology is making it not only possible but also imperative for an increasing number of us to work from or close to our homes. The growth of the use of personal computers, sophisticated telephone systems, fax and the like allows us to communicate with each other with almost the same ease as we did when we worked in the same office, and at a fraction of the cost. In other words, we will not have to 'go to work', the work will come to us.

In future, if the forecasters are to be believed, offices as we know them will become things of the past. We will either be operating on our own with instant access to all the data we need to make our day-to-day decisions, or within small networks which will communicate with other networks through computers. Only a few core workers will be needed to run a small centralised office.

What will happen to meetings in this brave new world? Will they still be needed, or will it be possible to run organisations without them? If so, what might replace them?

As I am not a futurologist, I would not like to make any predictions, but it is my belief that meetings will be even more essential than they are now. The very fact that people will be working alone with their technology rather than with other people will demand that they get together from time to time to make decisions and solve problems as they did in the past. Networks will also depend on regular exchanges of information, and this can only be done through meetings.

How people get together will be different – already the video meeting where people thousands of miles apart are able to sit in the same 'room' and talk to each other through satellite television is a fact of life for some large international corporations – but the need to do so will remain the same.

The rules, no doubt, will change. So, too, will the duties of Chairs and members. It will be interesting to see, for instance, how the Chair of a video meeting copes with the persistent interrupter. Perhaps she simply switches him off!

Work as we know it will not be the same and though technology will provide solutions to many of the problems that beset management today, it will also create new problems that will demand new solutions. Meetings will be challenged to resolve complex human issues the likes of which we cannot predict.

The future is much closer than we think . . .

12 How did the meeting go?

Twenty questions to ask yourself

■ *As Chair*

1 What was my purpose in calling the meeting? Was it to make a decision or to solve a problem? Was it to negotiate, to motivate, to create ideas, to train, to build a team, or a mixture of some of these? Whatever the reason, did I know what it was?

2 Could I have achieved the same results by another less expensive, time-consuming way; for instance, if it was to convey information to the members, could I perhaps have sent a letter or memo instead?

3 What were my reasons for inviting the members? Were they all essential, or was I asking some of them just to make myself look important and enhance my own reputation? Were there too many or too few, or did I get it just right?

4 Did I give them plenty of notice, and were other important documents sent well in advance so that they could prepare themselves?

5 Was the time and place for the meeting convenient for all? Was it held when the members were at their most lively and responsive, or late in the day and at the end of the week when they were tired and wanting to go home? If travel arrangements were difficult, did I send a detailed map of the venue?

6 Had I satisfied myself that the venue was prepared for the meeting: that the lighting was adequate, the room was quiet and free of distractions, the furniture pleasant but not too comfortable, that the seating allowed everyone to see me and each other clearly, and that the visual aid equipment was working?

7 Did I draw up a proper agenda? Did I work out the order of the items according to their importance, and did I know how long each item would take? Did I know how long the meeting would last?

8 If the meeting was formal or semi-formal, did I check on the rules and procedures, or was there someone at the meeting, the secretary for example, whom I could rely on to help me should I need to refer to them?

9 Had I worked out my meeting strategy? Were there any cliques or conspiracies or did any of the members have their own agendas that I should have known about? If so, was I ready to deal with them?

10 Had I given thought to how I presented myself? Were my clothes appropriate, and did my behaviour, facial expressions, posture and gestures convey the impression that I was confident, purposeful and businesslike?

11 Did I get the meeting off to a brisk start? Did I say how long it would last? Did I introduce new members or visitors to the others?

12 If I was nervous, was it obvious to the members, or did I cope with it adequately, concentrating on the issues and not on myself?

13 Were some members in need of particular attention and did I make use of non-verbal communication to give it, e.g. looking discouragingly at the talkers and encouragingly at the silent?

14 Did I need a secretary to take notes, or did I take my own while still giving my undivided attention to the meeting? For an informal meeting, did my notes include the reasons for the decisions or only the decisions? For a formal meeting, were they sufficient for the secretary to draw up the minutes?

15 Did I give everyone a fair hearing and an equal chance to express their views? Did I listen more than I spoke, and did I thank members after they had made their contributions?

16 Were there any problems and, if so, did I cope adequately with them? Was I able to maintain control and did I remain calm

throughout? Did I use techniques such as summarising to get the members back on track if they strayed?

17 Did the meeting achieve what it set out to do? Was a consensus reached? If not, was it because I did not leave sufficient time to summarise the issues clearly?

18 Did we finish on time? If not, was it because I interfered too much in the discussion or allowed some of the members to talk for too long? Will I be able to learn from my mistakes to improve my time-keeping at subsequent meetings?

19 Have I made sure that, as soon as possible after the meeting, the minutes or the record of the meeting were sent to the members together with any relevant documents?

20 Have the tasks I agreed to do after the meeting, and those undertaken by other members, been completed?

■ *As a member*

1 Why was I invited to the meeting? Was it because I was a member of a group, or had some particular expertise, or because of my status? Or did the Chair need my support? The reasons for the invitation could affect the way I prepared myself.

2 When I received the notice of the meeting, did I inform the Chair or the secretary whether or not I could attend, and did I note down the date in my diary?

3 If the meeting was being held away from the office, and I was unsure how to get there, did I ask for clear directions so that I would not arrive late?

4 Had I read through any documents that were sent to me before the meeting, and if I was expected to introduce, or talk on, a subject, did I undertake further research so that I was properly prepared?

5 Was the agenda also sent and, if so, did I go through it carefully, marking those items I wanted to speak on? Did I make notes so that I could refer to them when I spoke and not waste the meeting's time while I struggled to make my point?

6 Did I inform my secretary or others that I was not to be disturbed while I was at the meeting?

7 Did I regard myself as one of the 'welcomed' members, i.e. did I go intending to make a positive contribution to the meeting, to concentrate on all the issues, and to add my voice to the debate where it would assist in bringing the meeting to a consensus? Or –

8 Was I using the meeting for my own purposes? Did I have a hidden agenda that was more important to me than the reason for which the meeting was called?

9 Did I arrive on time, and was I happy with the way I presented myself? Did I conduct myself in a friendly manner? Was I in a positive frame of mind, and ready to get started?

10 Did I remember to bring with me the copy of the agenda and any accompanying documents?

11 Were my contributions relevant, brief and to the point, or did I speak for too long and go off the subject? Did I speak in a confident voice and with conviction, or nervously and uncertainly?

12 Was I calm and in control even when under attack from other members? Did I concentrate on the issue under discussion and refrain from personal abuse?

13 Was I supportive of the Chair, helping to bring the meeting back on track by summarising or asking the right question at the appropriate moment?

14 Was I concentrating throughout on what was being said, and was this clear from the manner in which I sat and made eye contact with the Chair and the other members? Or –

15 Did I let my attention wander, revealing my inattentiveness by the way I gazed around the room, doodled on my pad or slouched in my chair?

16 Did my contributions help the meeting reach a consensus within the time allotted, or was I deliberately negative and obstructive, and did I become hostile and aggressive if my viewpoint was not upheld?

17 Did I enjoy myself? Did I put into the meeting as much as I got out of it? Did I feel that as a result of the way I spoke, looked and behaved I was an active participant and contributed to the success of the group as a whole?

18 When volunteers were called for to carry out tasks after the meeting, did I indicate my keenness to do so, or did I let others volunteer?

19 Was I sensible in taking on only what I knew I could do properly, or was I too eager to make an impression and burden myself with tasks I would have difficulty performing?

20 Did I let my enthusiasm wane after the meeting and procrastinate until I lost interest in what I had agreed to do, or did I carry out the tasks promptly?

All the checklists

Checklist

Good reasons for having meetings

☐ To bring people together

☐ To aid communications

☐ To inspire

☐ To energise

☐ To pool resources

☐ To liberate

☐ To get you noticed

☐ Meetings are natural

Bad reasons for having meetings

☐ To avoid responsibility

☐ To display power

☐ Out of habit

☐ To avoid work

☐ To avoid writing

☐ To rubberstamp decisions

Checklist

The characteristics of the ideal Chair

The ideal Chair should have:

- ☐ Flexibility

- ☐ Confidence

- ☐ Authoritativeness

- ☐ Fairmindedness

- ☐ Ability to listen

- ☐ Self-discipline

- ☐ A good sense of humour

- ☐ Familiarity with rules of procedure

- ☐ Fun being a Chair

Checklist

How to be effective as a Chair

☐ Present yourself effectively

☐ Be in control

☐ Be visible

☐ Be alert

☐ Be a good listener

☐ Be humble

☐ Encourage fair play

☐ Be unafraid

☐ Be yourself

Checklist

How to be an effective member

- ☐ Come prepared to the meeting

- ☐ Speak clearly and to the point

- ☐ Be a good listener

- ☐ Be tactful and polite

- ☐ Be patient

- ☐ Be unafraid

- ☐ Be supportive to the Chair

- ☐ Do not misuse the meeting

Checklist

What makes a good secretary?

☐ Intelligence and clear-thinking

☐ A good memory

☐ The ability to organise

☐ Enjoyment of meetings

☐ The right status

☐ A calm personality

☐ Friendliness

☐ The right skills

☐ Being a good listener

☐ Open-mindedness and fairness

☐ Being well informed

☐ Clairvoyance

Checklist

The ideal venue

☐ A rectangular room

☐ With sufficient space to accommodate everyone in comfort

☐ Quiet

☐ Well lit

☐ Airy

☐ With good acoustics

☐ Free from interruptions

☐ Pleasantly decorated

☐ Available

☐ In easy communication with the outside world

☐ Conveniently situated

☐ Available at a reasonable cost

☐ Agreeable to everyone present

Checklist

Calling the meeting

Chair

☐ Check diaries

☐ Telephone or send written notice

☐ Send agenda and accompanying documents

Members

☐ Note details of meeting

☐ Notify non-attendance

☐ Arrange travel